— • —

Having a Life

Self-Pathology After Lacan

— • —

Having a Life

Self-Pathology After Lacan

Lewis A. Kirshner

THE ANALYTIC PRESS
2004   Hillsdale, NJ   London

Published by The Analytic Press, Inc.
101 West Street, Hillsdale, NJ 07642
www.analyticpress.com

An earlier version of chapter 6 was previously published in *Imago*, Volume 60, number 2, and appears here by permission of the publisher.

"The Self" from WITHOUT END: NEW AND SELECTED POEMS by Adam Zagajewski, translated by Clare Cavanagh, Renata Gorczynski, Benjamin Ivry and C. K. Williams. Copyright © 2002 by Adam Zagajewski. Translation copyright © 2002 by Farrar, Straus and Giroux, LLC. Reprinted by permission of Farrar, Straus and Giroux, LLC.

Typeset in Sabon 11/13 by EvS Communication Networx, Point Pleasant, NJ
Index by Writers Anonymous, Inc., Phoenix, AZ

Library of Congress Cataloging-in-Publication Data

Kirshner, Lewis A., 1940–
    Having a life : self pathology after Lacan / Lewis A. Kirshner.
      p. cm.
    Includes bibliographical references and index.
    ISBN 0-88163-401-8
    1. Self psychology. 2. Intersubjectivity. 3. Psychoanalysis. 4. Lacan, Jacques, 1901– I. Title.

RC489.S43K57 2004
155.2—dc22   2003057939

Printed in the United States of America
10 9 8 7 6 5 4 3 2 1

To Adam, Phebe, Ben, Sarah, Sabine, and Freddi:
L'Chaim!

The Self

—◆—

It is small and no more visible than a cricket
in August. It likes to dress up, to masquerade,
as all dwarfs do. It lodges between
granite blocks, between serviceable
truths. It even fits under
a bandage, under adhesive. Neither customs officers
nor their beautiful dogs will find it. Between
hymns, between alliances, it hides itself.
It camps in the Rocky Mountains of the skull.
An eternel refugee. It is I and I,
with the fearful hope that I have found at last
a friend, am it. But the self
is so lonely, so distrustful, it does not
accept anyone, even me.
It clings to historical events
no less tightly than water to a glass.
It could fill a Neolithic jar.
It is insatiable, it wants to flow
in aqueducts, it thirsts for newer and newer vessels.
It wants to taste space without walls,
diffuse itself, diffuse itself. Then it fades away
like desire, and in the silence of an August
night you hear only crickets patiently
conversing with the stars.

ADAM ZAGAJEWSKI

Contents

—◆—

Acknowledgments

— —

THIS BOOK WAS A LONG TIME IN GESTATION AND MANY COLLEAGUES AND friends have helped along the way. My participation in the Lacanian Forum over many years under the leadership of John Muller introduced me to Lacanian thinking. The invitation of André Green to attend the annual colloquia of the Paris Psychoanalytic Society helped me to appreciate his contributions, as well as those of many French colleagues. Teaching at the Université de Lyon 2 in the Department of Clinical Psychopathology, where I was able to work with René Roussillon and other distinguished faculty members, was also invaluable in broadening my frame of reference. Long conversations with the late Jacques Hassoun, André Michels, and Paola Mieli enlightened me about Lacanian theory and practice. Arnold Modell has been generous with time and encouragement. Other important readers and colleagues include Sabine Giesbert, James Frosch, Peter Lawner, Harry Penn, Andrew Morrison, Peter Rudnytsky, Dominque Scarfone, Paul Israël, Jean and Monique Cournut, and other members of my francophone study group. Jacques Mauger of Montreal and I have co-led a discussion group on clinical applications of Lacanian theory to practice at meetings of the American Psychoanalytic Association over many years. Paul Stepansky provided valuable editorial advice and Meredith Freedman helped get my final manuscript into publishable shape. Finally, I thank the staff at the IMEC archives in Paris for their help with my research on Louis Althusser.

Having a Life

Self-Pathology After Lacan

Introduction

— ◆ —

IN THIS BOOK I FOCUS ON A LACANIAN QUESTION: HOW DOES A PERSON support his or her separate existence as a subject? How, that is, does he or she sustain a vital presence as a speaking being against all the many forces that fragment, negate, and depersonalize? Although Lacan deserves credit for directing attention to this crucial issue of the subject in analytic work, numerous other theorists using the vocabularies, variously, of ego integrity, identity, and self have also touched on the problem, which has recaptured contemporary interest through the perhaps overused concept of intersubjectivity. The fragile or vulnerable self of Kohutian analysis that is so much the focus of clinical attention today (and with good reason) is a familiar example of this reorientation of clinical theory. This leads me to wonder what it is about "having a life" that we usually take for granted but that is lacking or so vulnerable to doubt in some patients and perhaps for most reflective people at difficult times. More broadly, I would like to explore what reading Lacan can offer us as a critique or supplement to the English language authors with whom North American analysts are most familiar and who have provided most of our understanding of the clinical issues raised by patients complaining of this problem.

Aside from its purely philosophical references, intersubjectivity in psychoanalytic theory has been a corrective to a naive view of the natural emergence of a "self" from a series of inborn matura-tional processes engaging a normal expectable social environment— a fallacy that collapses all that is unique and mysterious about culture and the way it provides identities and roles for human beings in the interest of fitting into a narrow psychobiology. Against this

1

reductionistic conception, intersubjectivity has emphasized the social field organized by the symbolic framework of language, which
makes the "self" a much more tenuous and vacillating sort of entity than we like to think. It is this point upon which Lacan, in
taking up his reading of Freud, insisted over and over again throughout his career.[1] Yet, as its tendency to overuse demonstrates, the
term intersubjective can be endowed with many meanings, including a simplistic one that seems to reify the notion of self and suggests the possibility of a full and complete relationship, a notion
that Lacan consistently rejected.[2] So we remain in need of a more
careful explanation of the concept of intersubjectivity, especially
in relation to psychotherapeutic practice.

   Lacan is known for his prodigious effort to open psychoanalysis
to a dialogue with other "human sciences" such as linguistics, philosophy, and anthropology, which his biographer, Roudinesco
(1993), sees as his greatest achievement. He may have been the
first to bring the age-old problem of the subject to the foreground
of analytic practice and to emphasize its divided and shifting nature, split by language, but his contribution is often cryptic and
demands both unpacking and revision in the light of other major
theorists. English-speaking analysts, of course, generally refer to
"the self" in their writings, avoiding the technical and experimen-
tal connotations of the term "subject," which may come easier to
users of romance languages. However, the use of an apparent substantive, the self, can lead to misconceptions, among which is a
quasireligious idealization of some soullike essence inside the person. The same may be said for Erikson's earlier concepts of identity and ego identity. For this reason, these latter terms have been
objects of criticism by many Lacanians, who detect in them a level
of psychoanalytic naivete, if not a malign will to social engineer-
ing, that has provided an "other" to these embattled but numerous analytic dissidents.

   It is not my purpose to delve into the history of these various
terms, which continue to play a political role in psychoanalytic
circles. I would merely observe that the conceptions of the ego

---

[1]Lacan (1953–1954) developed his notions of intersubjectivity at some length in
Seminar 1, *Freud's Papers on Technique*, one of his most accessible presentations.
[2]See, for example, Lacan's (1959–1960) satirizing of the concept of intersubjectivity, in which he portrayed a kind of mutual narcissistic manipulation
game.

psychologists, Erikson's theories of identity, and Kohut's use of self are much more subtle than these critics usually allow.[3] The question, however, is not the truth or error of any of these necessarily incomplete theories, but, I suggest, their sharing an at once scientific (psychological) and clinical quest to grasp conceptually the elusive object of psychoanalytic practice—the ineffable nature of the unique named human being who lives within a universe structured from birth to death by language and who is capable of possessing and losing a sense of permanence and embodiment. Although these terms map onto somewhat different traditions, I believe that both subject and self are attempts to grasp the true signified of our analytic work, perhaps better captured by Freud's ambiguous use of *Ich* or "I" than by the narrower, artificial term Ego.

In many respects, as Green (1975, 1999) consistently and cogently argued, contemporary psychoanalysis has undergone a major transformation in which primary conceptual and therapeutic attention has been redirected toward the origins of the self and the maintainance of its sense of aliveness and engagement in the world. Modell (1993) proposed this paradigm shift as one replacing Freud's structural theory, that *deuxiéme topique* of the French. One often hears this new focus on the subject/self attributed to a change in the pathologies of psychic life, perhaps the result of increasing social disorganization and the decline of stable communities that have undermined the formation of strong personal identities. The great structuring institutions of family and religion, which traditionally anchored the self in moral and ethical principles, have lost much of their vigor, whereas the questioning of norms in sexuality and gender, along with much greater freedom and opportunity for the pursuit of personal pleasure, have loosened the wrappings of identity and modified the old ideals and limits that structured the Western subject. All these changes have created a cultural ground increasingly alien to the context in which psychoanalysis originally evolved, one that conceived of individuals as autonomous centers with firmly delineated boundaries and contained psychic spaces. The recognition that people are much less crisply defined and in many respects permeable to other subjects with whom they are in interaction

---

[3]Lacan's critique of ego psychology is rampant in his *Écrits* (1966) but is presented more readably in *The Seminar Book II* (1954–1955), in which he attacked Erikson's developmental model. See Miller (1987) for a Lacanian critique of Kohut.

has transformed our understanding of the treatment situation, which we now understand as an intersubjective experience structured by what the analyst brings to it and by the evolution of the new relationship established. Perhaps our clinical understanding has surpassed our theoretical explanations, the latter still enmeshed in models of the mind that have in many respects outlived their usefulness.

At the same time, in the present state of affairs we are saturated with newer concepts and models that lack mutual articulation. Although Winnicott was far from a systematic theoretician, he is increasingly the object of our attention and will be central to our inquiry. Kohut and self psychology transformed the American analytic landscape, and in France Lacan rewrote the book in his circuitous "return to Freud." These authors rarely mention one another, although many parallels leap out for the attentive reader, as I will try to point out. Fortunately, we have other important thinkers to help us, notably Arnold Modell, whose *Psychoanalysis in a New Context* (1984) bridged Winnicott and object relations with American ego psychology and contemporary philosophical currents, and André Green, who performed a similar function in relation to Lacan. Both Modell and Green remained strongly committed to a Freudian heritage.

I see this present work as continuing a mediation between contemporary practice and these theoretical currents as they touch on the central existential and clinical problem of the fragile subject or, in the American idiom, the enfeebled, weakly cohesive self. My goals are to draw out some common threads from these varied discourses that may be useful to weave into a newer model of psychotherapeutic work and to contribute to the evolution of psychoanalysis away from a neurobiological or mechanistic reductionism, while safeguarding its indispensable features from too cozy a relationship with the dominant cultural ideologies. Often, it seems, the disappointed or embarrassed turn away from Freudian metapsychology, most of which has failed to hold up in fulfilling its goals as a scientific framework and has left analysts clinging to scraps of theories or a reliance on the beneficent aspects of the two-person relationship involved.[4] Although this tendency some-

---

[4]A recent publication by a team of market researchers hired by the American Psychoanalytic Association reported that analysts see themselves as empathic, engaged helpers, who "support the individual in his or her struggle to become the whole self" (Zacharias, 2002, p. 5). Analysis was described as "a relationship

times approaches the caricature attacked by Lacan with some vitriol in his assaults on the conformism and social adjustment allegedly supported by American psychoanalysts, I do not share his viewpoint "against adaptation" (the title of Van Haute's [2002] recent interpretation of Lacanian theory). I am certainly not attempting to represent a rigorous Lacanian view, which often ends up simply rehashing the difficult rhetoric. Rather, I want to provide a reading of Lacan through my American-trained, Freudian lenses for what it can offer clinicians interested in understanding more about their patients and themselves. *Adaptation to Life*, the title of George Vaillant's (1977) important study of male development, is a good term to describe the process of sustaining a self, and his book was a major influence on my own clinical thinking. Nonetheless, the language of adaptation may be too compromised at this point, the vocabulary of ego psychology too mechanistic, so that we need to move on to other, hopefully richer, ways of pursuing the development of psychoanalysis.

I believe that Lacan still has much to teach us in this respect, despite his notorious obscurity and the absence of detailed clinical accounts in his writings. He mainly reinterpreted, sometimes brilliantly, the published cases of others. Although many people think of him as more literary philosopher than therapist, Lacan was engaged principally in the practice of psychoanalysis his entire life, and his theories seem to have been motivated to a great extent by his dissatisfaction with then current practices. It is from this angle, in fact, that I wish to approach his writings, leaving the assessment of his vast theoretical project to others better qualified than I.[5] The other major thinkers on whom I draw—Winnicott, Kohut, Modell,

---

in which one can reveal his or her deepest secrets." Apart from the obvious public relations slant of these statements and their echoes of contemporary pop psychology, one might wonder what these analysts believe they have to offer over any other empathic, helping relationship?

[5]The results are surely mixed at this point and touched by polemic. Especially in France, it may still be too soon to expect a balanced assessment. For critical readings of Lacan, see Roustang (1986) and Borch-Jacobsen (1990). For a mainstream Freudian overview of his contributions, see Diatkine (1997). Van Haute (2002) provides a remarkably clear and sympathetic explanation of one important Lacanian text, which also touches many related topics. Roudinesco (1993) undertakes an assessment of Lacan's *oeuvre* in her biography, especially highlighting his intellectual accomplishments. Perhaps the best introduction to Lacanian theory and practice for North American clinicians is Fink (1997).

and Green—tend to be more experience and clinically near, and all attempted to revise basic psychoanalytic concepts, especially those concerning the basic issues of existence with which I am dealing. The contributions of Arnold Modell and André Green have been particularly helpful to me in this effort. In the following chapters, I develop some of the fruits of my readings of these authors, and offer a synthesis of theory in an attempt to indicate possible answers to the questions I have raised. Against Lacan, I argue for the central function of affect as knitting the individual to the social framework that anchors subjective existence. I see affect not simply as concerned with fantasies and images but as a symbolic activity that provides modes of expression able to be intersubjectively shared and communicated. In this respect, I propose a reinterpretation of Freud's concept of the ego ideal, suggesting that it functions to mediate private experience with narrative models provided by the culture. These models carry ideals and values that channel self-experience away from purely narcissistic preoccupations and thereby protect against the fragmentation of self described from different perspectives by Kohut and Lacan.

In chapter 1, I discuss Winnicott's analysis of Margaret Little, in order to illustrate the clinical problem that is my theme and to lay out some of the crucial issues in treatment. Chapters 2, 3, and 5 address theoretical issues raised by Lacan and others (always attempting not to lose sight of the clinical reference point). I try to maintain a dialogue between Kohut and Lacan, who I see as aiming at a common clinical object, despite the divergence of their two theories. Throughout, I attempt to sustain an anthropological perspective on human behavior as a corrective to the narrowness of cultural vision that I believe constricts psychoanalysis today. To further illustrate my ideas, I present two extended cases in chapter 4 and a briefer one in chapter 5. Finally, in chapter 6, I use material from the autobiographical writings of Louis Althusser as another point of entry into the problem with which I began: What makes it possible to be the subject of one's own desire and to sustain a personal existence—to have a life?

1

The Case of Margaret Little

> *"My real problems were matters of existence and
> identity: I did not know what 'myself' was."*
> —MARGARET LITTLE

THE WORDS OF THE ARTIST AND PSYCHOANALYST MARGARET LITTLE CON-
vey a problematic uncertainty to her sense of existence and a difficulty sustaining a subjective position in the world that is echoed by
many patients—the complaint of "not having a life." Little (1985)
described what Kohut would later call a pathology of the self, a
self for whom, in her terms, "anxieties concerning existence, survival, or identity" (p. 15) predominate. Little's first analyst in the
late 1930s had observed that she seemed to doubt her own right to
existence. Modell was to address this issue in a groundbreaking
paper of 1965, "On Having the Right to a Life." He was here
building on Winnicott, who was to become Margaret Little's third
analyst, by returning to a study of the effects of disturbances in the
earliest object relations. Modell described patients whose inability
to accept successes and pleasures in their lives betrayed a powerful
antiself dynamic, a basic guilt in establishing themselves as separate individuals from the maternal object. Separation for them
meant unconsciously a destructive attack on the mother, from whom
something valuable was being wrenched, perhaps analogous to
Klein's notions about infantile envy. Modell did not limit his analysis
to serious psychopathological states, but suggested that such guilts
and fears formed a part of many patients' conflicts.

Although Little might have said that her problems were not
about "having a right," but about having any existence at all (in
fact, she did say something quite similar), the two questions are

linked. Having a right to a separate self means renouncing the one-ness of a mother–child dyad or, what amounts to the same thing in a Lacanian framework, renouncing the possibility of satisfying the Other's desire and moving toward an assumption of one's own (separate) desire.[1] This passage was exactly what Little was unable to complete, unable to experience a second, psychic birth as a separate, desiring self. The important British psychologist and theorist, Harry Guntrip, was to seek out Winnicott for reasons quite similar to her's after an impasse in his first analytic experiences. For these two damaged individuals, something had gone awry in early life experience which they could not name; something was missing for which words were just beginning to be found when they first consulted him. Perhaps they demonstrate, in ways that go beyond their particular circumstances, the widening gap in the postmodern subject between desire and intersubjective identity caused by a tearing of the social fabric into which individual subjectivity is knit. The Lacanian social theorist, Žižek (1994), argues that the destabilization of traditional values and ideologies during the postwar period carried to an extreme the monadic isolation of the bourgeois self in European societies. For many vulnerable persons, psychoanalysis as a social institution—during these fecund years of its history—offered the possibility of repair or restitution of a damaged or alienated self. Guntrip's saga is exemplary in this respect. His quest for personal meaning led him from a protestant Christian calling as a minister toward psychoanalysis as a vehicle for restoration of the pure, natural self he sought. His French contemporary, the philosopher Louis Althusser, initially inspired by Lacan, turned to analysis for very similar reasons, experiencing a lack of personal existence that haunted his life. His disillusionment with the Catholic faith and communist ideology that had organized his intellectual and emotional life and his unremitting search for a set of viable ideals are vividly portrayed in his autobiographical writings, which I discuss in chapter 6. The theme of self-restoration was, of course, explicitly taken up by Kohut, who in many ways echoed the liber-

---

[1]The entire subject of separation leading to the second birth of the human subject is circumnavigated again and again by Lacan, for example, in "The Subversion of the Subject and the Dialectic of Desire" (1960) and in Seminar IV (1956–1957). That is, it is approached indirectly and often through the negative. Van Haute (2002) has attempted to translate these passages into a more "experience near" and user friendly manner (see pp. 104–119).

ating post-Freudian zeal of Guntrip in an American setting. There was passion as well in Lacan's commitment to probing the secrets of the human subject. Like Kohut and Guntrip, he rejected the mechanistic model of ego psychology, defending a more dynamic depiction of psychic life that he found in Freud.[2] Perhaps Freud could explore the mechanisms of the mind during an earlier, more stable era without immediately bringing into question the secure identity of the European bourgeois evoked by Žižek. Winnicott's interests were in many ways parallel to Lacan's, particularly his attention to the origins of self within the mother–child relationship, and it was the application of his ideas to patients like Margaret Little and Guntrip that aroused so much interest[3] in his writings.

Little (1985) writes of her first session with her second analyst, Ella Freeman Sharpe, that she lay rigid on the couch, unable to speak or move. Later she began to scream. After sitting her up, Sharpe interpreted her fear as a kind of castration anxiety resulting from a rivalry for the affections of Little's previous male analyst, whom she also knew. Little disagreed, arguing that her fear was one of "utter destruction, being bodily dismembered . . . wiped out" (p. 14). Later, she was to make a misattunement of this type by Dr. Sharpe the centerpiece of her important article on countertransference (Little, 1951). There are similiarities in her description of Sharpe to Guntrip's (1975) well-known account of his first analysis with Fairbairn. In both cases, a dedicated and caring analyst behaved rather rigidly and silently, sticking to oedipal interpretations. Of course, Fairbairn went much further in the direction Guntrip sought and was already breaking with analytic orthodoxy. In some ways he was ahead of Winnicott.[4] Both analysts no doubt helped their difficult and challenging patients considerably, but a residue was left, a fundamental untouched residue that led both eventually to the couch of D. W. Winnicott. Little was later to diagnose her relationship to Sharpe as a transference psychosis based on earliest infancy. This situation was certainly repeated and even fostered in her subsequent analysis with Winnicott, who believed

---

[2]Kohut (1977) mentioned Lacan with others as overlapping with his own interests.
[3]Rudnytsky's (1991) comparative study of Kohut, Lacan, and Winnicott deals with many issues touched on in this chapter.
[4]See Winnicott and Khan's (1953) review of Fairbairn, in which the lonely Scotsman was tarred with the accusation of departing from Freudian theory.

that regression was necessary and was prepared to accept it. She once again lay silent in their first session, where Winnicott commented that she was shutting him out for some reason, a true object relations interpretation of the experience of self with other. Modell (1980) would elaborate this phenomenon in his paper, "Affects and Their Non-Communication," in which he observed the defensive need of certain patients to shut the analyst out to protect a vulnerable self against a repetition of traumatic early maternal failure. Green (1975) had offered an analogous hypothesis, in which he spoke of an impossible attempt to abandon relations with objects, leading to a "negative hallucination of the self" (p. 55), like Little's belief in her nonexistence. Guntrip may have accomplished the same result of distancing his analyst by his pressured talking during the sessions. These tactics of noncommunication suggest an underlying fantasy of a powerful, uncaring or dangerous, devouring mother, who must be shut out at all cost.

Little's account of her treatments brings out two of the important dimensions of the emergence of subjective life in infancy emphasized by André Green—the problematics of presence (her frightening quasihallucination of Sharpe as a kind of spider), evoking the danger of being devoured or destroyed by the object, and of absence (feeling out of contact with Winnicott), threatening psychic annihilation by another who might not respond to what was most important to her. She desperately needed an object, not for pleasure, but for recognition and presence, yet feared being destroyed by misunderstanding or impingement. Modell (1990), describing a group of patients similar to Little, wrote that closeness can threaten the existence of the self, whereas distance may lead to deadness. Modell (1980) had observed that the fear of destruction by the failure of an empathic response may be met by a sort of nonrelatedness, inducing a reciprocal coldness in the analyst. Although his emphasis here was on the patient's anxiety and defensive maneuvers in the context of internal object relations, Modell's formulation was on the way to the two-person psychology that he was later to advocate. Now we would say that exploration of the analyst's unwitting or unconscious participation in this type of situation is an essential element of an effective treatment, not because it creates the patient's problem, but because it provides the road to understanding and reconstruction of a basic developmental and structural failure in which the analyst has inevitably been (re)playing a part.

In his scathing critique of analytic models of transference, Lacan (1958) mocked the metaphor of distance used by object relations analysts as implying a simplistic version of the two person psychology, in which the symbolic dimension of subjectivity is slighted in favor of an imaginary "real" relationship—"ripening the Object in the hot house of a confined situation" (p. 245). To my way of thinking, Winnicott is more enlightening here than Lacan, as he addresses the symbolic "maternal provision" and its failures. Winnicott may have overemphasized the maternal aspects of the patient's relationship to the Other (the analyst in the transference, the primordial mother, the symbolic order), whereas Lacan mistrusted the traumatic potential of maternal overpresence, which became the cornerstone of his theory of anxiety (see Harari, 2001). Rudnytsky has cleverly contrasted the difference between the two by suggesting the term "name of the mother" as Winnicott's equivalent of the important Lacanian concept *nom du père* (name of the father). Their disjunction on this point carried over to their respective conceptions of therapeutic action. Winnicott developed a model of regressive reliving of a damaging infantile situation and did not hesitate to establish his own active holding presence, whereas Lacan looked more toward making a decisive cut in the infantile dyad, allowing the patient to emerge as a differentiated subject of desire. As Eigen (1981) wrote, both shared the goal of enabling the subject to persevere in the difficult task of human existence.

Rudnytsky (1991) has further polarized Winnicott from Lacan by highlighting their different conceptions of self. Although his analysis of their complex and not always consistent ideas is nuanced, he comes down on the side of an "essentialist," core self as truer to human experience than the fissured and divided subject of Lacan and the postmoderns. He faults Lacanian theory for rupturing the wholeness that characterizes healthy personal experience (thus supporting Guntrip's position) and for replacing it with an inherently unstable and alienated self. Although acknowledging the fuzziness of Winnicott's notion of a "true self," Rudnytsky argues that it provides a more solid foundation for a renewed psychoanalysis, and he presents the image of a happy, self-realized Winnicott as a better model than the more tormented subject of Lacan. In my view, something is lacking in this picture, which seems more of an affirmation of one side of a duality than a complete theory, and is unfair to the complexity of both thinkers. Although Winnicott is certainly the more appealing psychoanalyst from what we know of their work, I believe that his buoyant optimism and belief in health, cited by Rudnytsky, needs balancing by the tragic vision of Freud and the structuralist antihumanism of Lacan. For this reason, I support Rudnytsky's other stated wish of "having Winnicott with Lacan" (p. 85).

The different emphases of Lacan and Winnicott are fairly clear and colored their clinical technique, where the comparisons are not necessarily in Lacan's favor. In general, he was critical of the analyst's departing from her formal role as support for, but not an active agent of, the transference, for which he advocated a traditional analytic position. Although he attacked the atomistic or essentialist model of an interiorized subject to be uncovered or liberated by the enlightened analyst (for example, by being raised to the level of genital object relations, already biologically inscribed in his or her destiny) and argued that the unconscious was not like a buried crypt to be excavated in treatment but a "transpersonal" construct (a term used in the "Rome Discourse" of 1953), Lacan's writings support an abstinent transference model quite unlike Winnicott's. His discussions of technique present a classic view of the analyst as providing a mirror, one if anything more austere than Freud's, reflecting the patient's own messages in a kind of dialectical operation. This use of the mirror metaphor further differentiated him from Winnicott and, later on, Kohut. Winnicott emphasized the infant's gaining a sense of his existence in the mother's eyes, enabling him to begin to perceive actively, whereas, for Kohut, mirroring meant a process of attunement by the parent to the child (or analyst to patient). In both versions, there was implicit recognition of the affective communication involved. In this regard, the role of affect was relegated entirely by Lacan to the imaginary transference[5] as a deception or lure to be overcome. Using his clever (but almost incomprehensible) analogy of psychoanalysis to a bridge game, Lacan (1958) spoke of the affective elements in

[5]Lacan went so far as to suggest suppression of the term *affective* from analytic vocabulary in Seminar I (1953–1954, p. 281). Borch-Jacobsen (1990) noted the absence of Freud's emphasis on the affective basis of the transference, as well as on the primary mother–infant relationship in Lacan's work (see pp. 77–93).

the transference as belonging to the analyst's position as the "dummy" (*le mort* or "the dead one," in French), using phrases like "the passive face of death" (p. 220).[6] He observed repeatedly the important function of frustration in mobilizing the patient's demands (behind demand, of course, the key element of desire), referring to the "terrible temptation" (p. 257) of the analyst to respond and contrasting analysis with the warmth of the ordinary human relationship.[7]

Although he may have implicitly accepted the framing and holding functions of an analysis, Lacan presents these more as an effect of the structure and setup of treatment than a product of the behavior of the analyst. A tendency to idealize the psychoanalytic situation as intrinsically therapeutic was also present in ego psychology and continues to play a part in contemporary psychoanalysis as well. In North America, what Green characterized as a maternalization of practice may account for the unquestioned assumption of its beneficent nature, as demonstrated by participants in the American Psychoanalytic Association's focus groups, who saw themselves as empathic, engaged helpers, working to "support the individual in his or her struggle to become the whole self" (Zacharias, 2002, p. 5). Lacan's emphasis on structure over process is illustrated by his invention of many schematic models, of which the schema L is notable, the point of which was to show the displacement of the analyst from any pretended role as subject of a "real" relationship into her necessary positions as object for the patient (as the dummy) and to the place she occupies of the Other. This was why he referred to the "pretended analytic situation," because it was not for him a true intersubjective situation.[8] The analyst, for Lacan, avoids all traps of responsiveness that might

---

[6]The dummy analogy was discussed in "The Direction of the Treatment and the Principles of Its Power" (Lacan, 1958), as well as in Seminar VIII (1960–1961), in which it was diagramed.

[7]In Lacan (1958), a highly calculated strategy of the treatment was presented.

[8]The full quote is

"indicating by this [pretended] some reference to the effort of these recent years in analysis to organise, around the the notion of a situation, what happens in analytic treatment. The word pretended is there best to say that I oppose myself, at least in a corrective position . . . to this attempt. I do not think that one may say of analysis, purely and simply, that there is a situation. If there is one . . . it is a false situation" [seminar of 16 November 1960; my translation].

support the ego and its imaginary transference, with the aim of taking the patient through his transference fantasies to the assumption of his own desire. To this end, the analyst accepts the essentially deceptive and even magical role of incarnating the symbolic Other, which will call forth the unconscious desire of the subject.[9]

Lacan's structural interpretation seems in many ways to support the classical, "objective" interpretive tradition, much as Freud advocated. One has only to read the accounts of his former patients offered by Roudinesco (1993), as well his own discussions of technique in which the "dialectical" returning of the patient's own message by the analyst was highlighted, to infer that the well-analyzed analyst can correctly read the patient's communications, respond to the important signifiers, and arrive at the correct designation of the ultimate interpretation, the *tu es cela* (thou art that; Lacan, 1949, p. 7). His controversial technique of punctuating (interrupting) sessions at the right moment seemed to imply an analogous capacity[10] for accurate judgment of when to intervene. While in theory the short sessions could have the impact of marking a point of intensity or of particular importance in the process—especially if the patient were prepared for such surprises—in practice, Lacan shortened the time to unjustifiably brief periods of only a few minutes, especially in his later years.[11] Contemporary Lacanians who practice the "scansion" of the analysand's discourse with this

---

[9]There are many versions of schema L, of which one pertaining to the transference was presented in Seminar VIII (Lacan, 1960–1961) and a fuller development was given in Seminar II (Lacan, 1954–1955). In this schema, Lacan depicted the interplay of the imaginary relation of the ego in the transference with its unconscious symbolic dimension. For more on the sorcery of the symbolic position assumed by the analyst, see Borch-Jacobsen (1990, pp. 190–201), where he underlined the essentially fictive nature of the symbol and of the patient's personal myth, received from the Other, which, for him, covers the emptiness of a being whose truest desire is for death. He concluded that Lacan aimed for the reinsertion of a confused subject into an arbitrary symbolic order via the recognition of signifiers of his own unconscious desire, which is essentially meaningless.

[10]One can pick up these indications of analytic mastery in Lacan's Seminar I (1953–1954), Seminar XI (1964), and in *Écrits* (1966), especially in "Direction of the Treatment" (1958). Much of Lacan's discussion of other analysts' work (see, e.g., his remarks on the case written up by Kris in "Direction of the Treatment") suggested a tone of certainty that would seem to directly contradict his own teaching.

[11]There are some scandalous and funny anecdotes recounted in Allouch's (1984) compendium. For example, an analysand sighed after a few moments, "I don't

theory in mind obviously make conscientious efforts to exercise their power judiciously, and, as a general rule, tend to use sessions of 25 to 30 minutes.[12]

There is an irony in this description of Lacan's practice. The excesses of "classic" psychoanalytic treatment in the direction of an assumed impersonality, commitment to some version of an objective or nonpersonally implicated functioning of the analyst, and avoidance of responsibility for the evolution of the transference relationship (already strenuously criticized by Ferenczi, 1933) have come to be identified with the mechanistic deviation of ego psychology from the vitality of an actively constructed, intersubjective encounter. As I have noted, it was certainly against this type of analysis, with its positivist ambitions, that Winnicott and Lacan were reacting in the late 1940s. Although few today would support any similar model of the analyst as presiding over an "untouched surgical field," it seems to me that psychoanalysts are still far from resolving or fully conceptualizing the tension between the classical doctor–patient (or, as Lacan scoffed, "shepherd–flock" paradigm) and the evolving relational and intersubjective model. In the former, the patient brings his troubled past, symptoms, and cumbersome ego for treatment; whereas in the latter, two subjects co-create a new, transformative experience. Again, something seems wrong with the exclusive choice of either of these alternatives, as polemicized by the different schools. So Lacan should not be singled out in this respect, even if, by seeming to incarnate, in Borch-Jacobsen's (1990) phrase, an "absolute master," he may have helped to perpetuate a mystifying and shamanistic style of psychoanalysis.[13]

At the same time, there is clearly another text in Lacan's writings

---

have anything to say." Lacan's amused response: "*Mais oui! Ça arrive. A demain cher*" (Of course, that happens. See you tomorrow). Or the analysand beginning, "I dreamt that . . ." interrupted by Lacan saying, "That's very good. See you tomorrow."

[12]I have discussed this problem informally with a number of Lacanians, notably the late Jacques Hassoun and, more recently, André Michels (both Parisian analysts). On one hand, the example of Lacan was followed, perhaps somewhat uncritically, by many of his students, just as Freud's has been. On a more theoretical level, Lacanians have concerns about emotional dependence on the analyst and on the tendency to regression by analysands, which raise interesting questions. Of course, many influenced by Lacan do not use the short sessions in their practices.

[13]For similar critiques of Lacan playing the part of master see Roustang (1986) and Althusser (1985a).

and lectures that undercuts the mastery of the analyst and that, moreover, provides important theoretical substance for an alternative model of the transference. One could say the same of Freud, of course, and, no doubt, there were historical reasons embedded in their epochs that explain why the revolutionary aspects of psychoanalysis as a liberating practice were grafted onto a version of paternal authoritarianism, only now slowly fading. Both men were freer and more spontaneous with their patients, more prone to enter into "enactments," which (in the best case) offer material to be used creatively to further the process, than a cursory reading might suggest. But Lacan went further than the scandalous freedom of speech and action often reported of him[14] by offering novel ways of conceptualizing the analytic relationship and by presenting a less constrained and socially repressive role for the analyst. In this regard, his discussion of countertransference in Seminar VIII (1960–1961) was ahead of its time by insisting that this phenomenon, beginning to be reevaluated contemporaneously by Paula Heimann and others, was an inevitable consequence of transference. The transference, he argued, depends on a speaking relation with another subject that, inevitably, incites unconscious desire, however well-analyzed the analyst. In fact, "the better the analyst is analysed, the more likely that he will be frankly in love or in a state of aversion and repulsion" (Lacan, 1960–1961, p. 224). In these passages, he acknowledged that something must be there for the patient besides the empty analytic mirror. Thus, in another of his cryptic but memorable parables, Lacan (1964) observed, "It is not enough that the analyst should support the function of Tiresias. He must also, as Apollinaire tells us, have breasts" (p. 270). Exploration of this avenue was bypassed, however, in favor of an emphasis on the ethics of the analyst's desire, which seems to amount to a desire for "absolute difference" (p. 276), a putative accomplishment of successful training analyses (and for him, there seem to be no other).[15] This ethic implicitly recognizes that the analyst cannot know the desire of the other and therefore is never in a

---

[14]Roudinesco (1993) gives examples. See also the anecdotes gathered by Allouch (1984) and Clement (1981).

[15]This formula is highlighted at the end of Seminar XI (Lacan, 1964). The entire discussion of countertransference in Seminar VIII (Lacan, 1960–1961) revolved around papers of Kleinian analysts, which seemed to evoke in Lacan an avuncular smile of tolerance for a kind of erroneous thinking (object relations) that has stumbled across a distorted truth.

position of knowledge from which to correctly interpret the unconscious of his patient. The metaphor of sustaining difference against the inevitable pressures of countertransference and the undeveloped notion of a "transpersonal" unconscious (Lacan, 1955), involving the interplay of two desires, capture for me the richness of Lacan's vision missing from Rudnytsky's critical evaluation.

In thinking about Lacan the analyst, particularly in developing his conception of the encounter of two subjects in analysis, it seems inevitable to wonder about his own analysis and his own desires to become an analyst. To a point that may have become excessive, no one today would discuss a case without reference to the previous analyst and his or her limitations. With all due reservations, this approach to Lacan's own classical analysis with Rudolph Loewenstein, the alleged failure of which is commonly attributed to Lacan himself, may at least situate his departure from the orthodoxy of the period in the context of analysis as it was then understood and practiced.[16] My hypothesis is that this training analysis left a traumatic residue influencing his own subsequent practice. There are indications, supported by Roudinesco (1993; Derrida and Roudinesco, 2001), that Lacan himself may have suffered early damage from an impoverished and rigid object environment, which left him with a vulnerability toward (and tendency to repeat) certain injurious experiences in later life.[17] Such a constellation may have been restaged in his several years-long training analysis of 1932–1938. Loewenstein, newly minted from the Berlin Institute, was a young man Lacan's age when he took him on as his patient, and it seems obvious that he lacked the seasoning and brilliance that a mature Winnicott was able to bring to bear on Margaret

---

[16]Roudinesco (1986, pp. 117–122) discusses this chapter of Lacan's history in her study of psychoanalysis in France and, more incisively, in her biography of Lacan (1993, pp. 70–74), where she cites interviews of colleagues and associates, as well as the biography of Marie Bonaparte by Bertin. For example, she recounts an incident described by Lacan in which he told his analyst about an incident in which he was driving his car in a tunnel toward a large oncoming truck, which ultimately gave way. Lacan allegedly understood this as a transference phenomenon about which Loewenstein failed to comment. In addition to the weight given this story by Lacan himself as describing a mortal Hegelian struggle with his analyst, the imagery of the tunnel also seems suggestive of Roudinesco's thesis of Lacan's damaged childhood.

[17]In addition to her accounts in the biography, Roudinesco uses the phrase "the psychic cruelty which marked the childhood of Lacan" (p. 299) in her fascinating dialogue with Jacques Derrida, *De quoi demain* (Derrida and Roudinesco, 2001).

Little and Harry Guntrip. The fact that Loewenstein, a creative
thinker and appreciated clinician in the heyday of post-war ego
psychology in America, was to devote his researches to the development of the ego as an organ of adaptation, while Lacan turned
toward the coming to be of the subject is doubtless significant.
Thus, Lacan translated Freud's (1933) famous dictum, "Where Id
was, there Ego shall be" (p. 80), as, "Where it was . . . it is my duty
that I must come into being" (Lacan, 1955, pp. 128–129). It is
surprising that no one has yet attempted to link Lacan's innovations with his own unsuccessful analytic experience, drawn like
most of us to repair his unresolved problems, which may have passed
unaddressed in the training analyses of the time.

According to Phillips (1988), Winnicott himself may have had
a "dead mother"—at least a depressed one whom he sought to
heal. Although his second wife, Clare, paints a picture of a happy,
secure childhood, there are indications that all was not rosy. Phillips
cites a late poem by Winnicott about his mother that includes the
lines, "Mother below is weeping, weeping, weeping. Thus I knew
her. Once, stretched out on her lap as now on a dead tree . . ."
(p.21). His wife did observe that a deliberate effort was made not
to spoil him, which may have deprived Winnicott "of some of the
intimacy and closeness he needed" (p. 22). Winnicott wrote that
after a youthful injury, he decided to become a doctor himself to
avoid depending on physicians in the future, and Clare observed
that he only became angry when he was ill. Possibly his choice of a
second analysis with a Kleinian, Joan Riviere, after 10 years with
James Strachey, was related to an unanalyzed piece of this early
problem of vulnerable passivity, which he was to address so brilliantly in this work with Guntrip. Riviere (cited in Phillips, 1988)
wrote that the analyst's concern was not "adaptation to the real
world" but "the imaginings of the childish mind" (p. 43).

A creative imperative to escape the restrictiveness of a stereotypic, oedipally focused psychoanalysis, congealed in the structures
of a declining patriarchal order, may have motivated both Lacan
and Winnicott to take new directions. A similar aversion to the
biologizing and reductionistic tendencies of ego psychology may
have contributed to Modell's innovations in his version of a two-
person psychology—for example, his advocacy of the crucial importance of the communication of affects in the dyad. Lacan saw
this avenue as headed toward the dead end of an idealized

intersubjectivity that ignores the presence of the symbolic order from which each subjectivity is suspended, but, as I have noted, his recognition of the intrication of two unconsciouses in analysis seems to point to another issue, one which, I believe, Modell and others have taken. In homage to Merleau-Ponty, Green (1973) observed that "affect is the signifier of the flesh and the flesh of the signifier" (p. 332). In Lacanian terms, it is the expression of the real in the play of two subjectivities. For me, the issue of the communication of affect raised by Modell is the crux of psychoanalytic therapy and is central to my approach in this book. It was certainly neglected by Lacan (or seen as derivative) and lacks development by Kohut, although both have something to teach us about affect. Although in some sense implicit in all of his writings, Winnicott also failed to say much on the subject. Of all the analysts with whom I will be dealing, only Modell and Green have systematically addressed the problem of affect in psychoanalytic theory, notably its signifying and communicating functions.

A central problem in this regard has been that psychoanalysts have tended to associate affect with the Id, with biology, and with a form of drive discharge, rather than seeing it as a symbolic activity. Thus they could aspire to an objective evaluation of the drive tensions. From my perspective, "having a life," the embodied feeling of personal existence, depends on the capacity to express affect in a form that can be communicated within a framework of shared meanings and social conventions that link the subject to others. I see the functions designated by the term *ego ideal* to be crucial to this process. The difficulty addressed by Green is that affect displays the features of force, intensity, and somatic arousal noted by Freud and seems to partake of something primal, biological, and preverbal in the infant–mother relationship, along the lines investigated by innovative researchers such as Daniel Stern (1985). At the same time, affect is intersubjective, structured, and communicative, as Stern also rightly insists. In speaking of these early life transactions between infant and mother, Stern infers a continuum of emotional expression ranging from pure discharge to highly patterned (learned) sequences that carry symbolic meaning. The latter view has been developed independantly by a number of anthropologists whom I discuss. These authors stress the cultural construction of affect, which implies both a particular form of self organization (a specific narrative of the self) and a familiar scene of action (a social paradigm). The transmission of cultural values and models, which Freud located in the parental superegos, then serves the function of structuring affect representations. When these symbolic links are lacking, affect remains uncommunicated or miscommunicated as flatness and deadness, or the obverse, as disruptive overflow.

There are many examples of disruptive affective discharge in Little's account. Once, in her despair that Winnicott could not understand her incommunicable feelings, she smashed a cherished vase, driving her analyst temporarily from the room. Later he admitted he had been hurt but thought that the act had been useful. Winnicott apparently did not interpret that the smashing of the vase might be an expression both of one pole of her experience in the transference (being destroyed or destroying) and of her self-state (as fragmented). Such an incident is not generally conducive to brilliant insights by any clinician, and Winnicott was in any event not too inclined to emphasize interpretation. Physical holding and attentive observation often took the place of verbal interventions with Little, perhaps brilliantly, as she clearly did not have the words at this point. The oscillation between explosion and silence is a familiar problem with many patients, as described by Green. I illustrate this with two extended case examples in chapter 4. Winnicott learned that, in fact, Margaret Little had been discouraged in childhood from expressing feelings. When he asked her why, she only cried silently. He recognized this as a failure in the mother–child holding and was able to reconstruct with her the damaging interactions with her mother, very much as he did with Guntrip. One might say that he was participatory (sometimes in rather intrusive ways, like meddling with Little's vacation plans by telephoning her friend), but did not analyze his participation, except as supplying a need. Today we might criticize him for this failure to explore his countertransference participation, despite the sensitivity of his intuition.

Little (1985) recounts an important series of events in her analysis after she had broken her ankle on a vacation trip to Scotland, following an "explosion" of anger toward her mother for the first time. Winnicott interpreted the accident as a suicidal reaction to separation from him, apparently having forgotten the important angry episode that preceded it. In her associations to this incident, Little referred to an illness around age five when she entered a febrile delirium, clinging desperately to her mother who, Winnicott interpreted, "would not let you die." Little amends this by saying, "she would not let me choose whether to live or die" (p. 31) Soon afterward, Winnicott himself took this role by insisting that she be hospitalized during his vacation, which she calls a repetition of his earlier reaction to her smashing the vase when he left her alone in the room. Her story suggests an odd confusion between intrusion (excess of presence) and abandonment (absence), restaging her infantile experience in the transference. The report reads as if Winnicott were attempting to supply a missing experience of good mothering, rather than to interpret the actuality of transference. Once admitted to the hospital, Little described undergoing a psychotic regression, at least one characterized by rages and childlike behavior, where she could again lose control, but in a safe environment. Upon discharge, she read her poems and recounted her hospital experiences to Winnicott "much as a child would tell its mother" (p. 84). Here the reparenting analogy was explicit.

In the terminal phase of her analysis, which followed closely upon release from the hospital, Little did receive an important interpretation to the effect that her fear of annihilation referred to an event that had already happened. Much as he was to describe in his paper, "Fear of Breakdown," Winnicott (1973) told her that she had already been psychically annihilated and was now reliving that experience. She agreed, saying that she had never been a person in her own right, only an appendage of someone else. Again, none of this was dealt with directly in terms of the analyst's role in the transference, at least according to Little's narration. Modell (1991) raised the important question, "whose reality is it?" in psychoanalysis, as there is always a danger of the well-meaning analyst imposing her own beliefs, goals, and values on the patient (which is why Lacan stressed "absolute difference"). The assessment of regressive phenomena is one important area in which this reality question can arise. Modell's position is that a patient can symbolically actualize a past relationship while preserving its "as if" character, different from the prototype. Transference is a new construction. Winnicott dealt with regression as though it were a true temporal return to an earlier state. In his short paper on countertransference (Winnicott, 1960), he differentiated neurotic patients toward whom the analyst maintains a symbolic distance—"the gap between the subjective object and the object objectively perceived"—and psychotic patients, who need to regress to a state of absolute dependency on the analyst. The analyst then responds to the patient's presumably real needs. Although Little is quite clear that for her the experience of her analyst as a "real" (that is, objective and separate) person was crucial to her recovery, she does not see him as a second mother. She felt privileged to have known and learned from Winnicott as an analysand and as a colleague in the British Psychoanalytic Society, and she reports that she came to accept what he could not give her of her frustrated infantile wishes.

Whether or not Winnicott did interpret the transference–countertransference enactments, including the possible effects of his own destructiveness, about which he wrote, it seems inescapable that some form of repetition of an earlier situation was a major dynamic of the analysis. As with Guntrip, he appears to have interpreted what the mother actually did or did not do, and he offered a substitute relationship in which earlier failures could be reexperienced and reworked. For these analysands, whose subjective cohesion and vitality were seriously compromised, he provided a holding frame and pointed to failures of environmental provision at the earliest phases of life. Probably, however, he also did something more and something less. Certainly he retained his place as a separate subject ("the desire of the analyst"), for example, telling Little his feelings about her poetry and artwork, whether he liked them or not. He was not necessarily empathic in the sense of attempting to achieve the patient's point of view, and he was not overly cautious in asserting his subjective reality. This stance would certainly have been approved of by Lacan, who insisted on noncompliance with patients' wishes for confirmation of their feelings in the transference. He would also have endorsed Winnicott's freedom to be himself and break with orthodoxy so that his patient might eventually rediscover her own desire as a separate subject. Although Lacan might have (hypocritically) condemned nonverbal interventions, which he himself was not too loathe to carry out, he would have been gratified to learn that it was some of the things Winnicott said that stuck with Margaret Little. Neither analyst apparently ever spoke much in the here and now of transference (although the evidence is incomplete on this point), perhaps in Winnicott's case because he did not feel that transference regression was an "as if" phenomenon that could be interpreted symbolically, especially in terms of his own participation. At the time both these men were trained (and the situation still persists to a great extent), all transference was viewed as a regressive product belonging to the patient, to be interpreted from outside by the analyst. Lacan realized that this type of objectifying interpretation was damaging (it was one of the breaks with orthodoxy for which he was severely criticized by the International Psychoanalytic Association's investigators [Roudinesco, 1986]), and he understood that the interaction (the intersubjectivity) was the crucial dimension of analytic practice. Unfortunately his own limitations may have prevented him from applying these theoretical innovations to clinical work, and he failed to offer the case material for others to learn from what Winnicott proffered.

It is of considerable interest to read Margaret Little's own published ideas about the countertransference, which were innovative and even revolutionary. In her 1951 article, published in the *International Journal of Psychoanalysis* while she was in treatment with Winnicott, she spoke about the constructive and necessary effects of the countertransference. She wrote that countertransference was not an obstacle to be analyzed but a predictable repetition by the analyst of an earlier relational position lived through in childhood by the patient. She advocated that the analyst communicate her experience, even if negative, as a means of shedding light on the past, which could then be reconstructed in the transference situation. The patient, she observed, lives her transference entirely in the present, while the analyst can potentially separate from this configuration and also see its origins. Psychoanalysis, she argued, creates a reverberating mirror situation for both participants based on transference, but over time, the images can become "clearer for both," as the analyst is able to reveal her subjectivity to the patient. Little also warned against the dangers of the analyst interpreting out of an unconscious countertransference, providing an extended example, which we can now see was derived from her first analysis with Sharpe. She attributed Sharpe's oedipal rivalry interpretation entirely to an unacknowledged countertransference. One wonders, however, whether this constructive use of the analyst's private experience was something Little missed in Winnicott as well. Perhaps his open style of interacting went part of the way for her in satisfying this therapeutic principle.

Lacan, as we have seen, was also interested in the countertransference, and, in fact, commented on Little's paper in his first seminar on technique (1953–1954). Unfortunately, rather than develop those aspects of her formulation that must have resonated with his own ideas, Lacan badly misinterpreted her position, attributing to Little a radical recentering of analysis in the *hic et nunc* (here and now). Although not as scornful as he could be about analytic authors, he did use Little as a representative of a misguided tendency he found in "the British school" to speak "ego to ego" (p. 32) with the patient. He also confused the anecdote about Sharpe's erroneous interpretation, first asserting that it was correct and then attributing it to Little herself with a candidate. Later, in a chapter once again taking up this theme, Lacan (1960–1961) described analysis as a relationship between two unconsciouses and distanced himself from the traditional view of the countertransference as a neurotic vestige. Two years later in his unpublished seminar on anxiety (1962–1963; see Harari, 2001), Lacan returned to the issue, reiterating his distorted reading of the *hic et nunc* theme. In some ways, both Winnicott and Lacan equivocated on the countertransference, Winnicott bracketing off the regressive phenomena in treatment of psychotics from the customary interpreting position of the analyst and Lacan still reiterating old saws about the well-analyzed analyst avoiding mistakes. Little saw more deeply, no doubt because of her own painful personal experiences, and helped initiate a paradigm change that we are still digesting.

All in all, one comes away from Little's moving account of her treatment with Winnicott with the impression of an enormously gifted analyst who had a grasp of the earliest building blocks of subjective organization (the mirror, transitional space, maternal preoccupation) and who was not afraid to cross boundaries and participate in a relationship. What, finally, may have helped her discover herself as a real person, existing in her own right? In my own clinical experience, which obviously is in no way comparable in depth or variety, the analytic holding environment and the benign role of a nurturant analyst, about which Winnicott taught us, have always seemed the basic foundation of all treatments. Beyond this, I share Rudnytsky's admiration for the way he was able to convey, if not always speak about, his own participation as an individual with her, distinct from his position as a "subjective object" created by her in the transference. Conversely, I have found transgressing boundaries to be uncomfortable and not necessarily useful (I refer to active interventions in patients' lives, touching, and other Winnicottian behaviors, of which, again, my own experience is much more limited). Winnicott is an inspiration, but not always a guide, and I miss a more elaborated theory, above all a theory of the "self" or subject. As Phillips (1988) notes, Winnicott's notions of the true self have essentialist connotations of an inborn core of a mystical nature.

In what follows, I take a closer look at the concepts of self and subject, attempting to relate the kinds of clinical phenomena addressed by Winnicott to broader themes. Probably, in the end, we will never know what made the difference for Margaret Little, yet with the help of Kohut, Modell, Green, and, of course, Lacan, I believe we can come much closer to understanding what is involved in the peculiar process of "having a life" and what had been missing for her that he was able to reestablish.

2

The Psychoanalytic Subject

*In the term subject . . . I am not designating the
living substratum needed by this phenomenon of the
subject, nor any sort of substance, nor any being
possessing knowledge in his pathos . . . but the
Cartesian subject, who appears at the moment when
doubt is recognized as certainty.*

—Jacques Lacan

LACAN'S WORK IN MANY WAYS REVOLVED AROUND THE ISSUE OF THE STATUS
of "the subject"—the Cartesian subject, who self-consciously knows
he exists. But he was not unique during his time in wanting to
refocus psychoanalysis on questions of identity, self, and existence,
as so diverse a group as Erikson, Winnicott, and Kohut demonstrates. The commonly voiced criticism that Lacan was behaving
more like a philosopher than a psychoanalyst in his seminars suggests the very complacency and banalizing tendencies that motivated his "return to Freud." For him, Freud was not simply a good
clinician with old-fashioned scientific ideas, but a revolutionary
thinker who exploded certain kinds of received wisdom about human beings, notably the belief in a unified subject or a self-directed
conscious ego that was (and is) fundamentally an extrapolation of
theological beliefs. Moreover, Freud proposed a model by which
conscious experience was the effect of unconscious mental structures, residues of otherness in ourselves (other subjects, inborn
patterns of relatedness, moral imperatives, drives, and so forth),
an otherness which Lacan separated from an imaginary biology of
the Id. Coded biological sequences might determine the behavior
of many species, but human life, as philosophers have always

27

puzzled about, seems to function by other rules and motivations with a peculiar status—motives like "pure prestige" or desires for recognition or for self-abnegation.

This is why analytic psychotherapy is mostly an ideographic discipline. It does not follow general rules of treatment applicable across the board to patients of one category or another, but focuses on the unique individual history that has produced a single patient. Cookbook assessments, abstract typologies of patients, or *DSM IV*-like attempts to match patients to specific treatments all miss the point if they stray too far from this principle. Even, in my opinion, the Lacanian tendency to refer to "the hysteric" or "the obsessive," although full of interesting observations, does not offer much direction in working with real cases.[1] Theory, although necessary for any understanding and modeling of what is happening clinically, has to be applied and worked with. Without theory, however, we are left in the equally precarious position of practicing ritualized techniques or applying some kind of ideology of help. Casting his net as broadly as possible to capture ideas beyond the Freudian paradigm of instinctual pressures, Lacan struggled with understanding important human questions. He probably broke more new ground than any other analyst after Freud (Melanie Klein may be one exception to this generalization), but he did not help us attach his theories to clinical practice. Especially since the matters concerning him were also approached by many others, we need to weigh his contribution with theirs.

In what follows, I trace a few major theoretical issues pertinent to the clinical problem of "having a life." I first discuss Lacan's conception of the mirror stage and its relationship to Winnicott and Kohut's use of the mirror metaphor, as well as his theory of the imaginary and symbolic orders. I then address the value and limitations of Kohut's stress on empathic responsiveness and the selfobject relationship. The symbolic function of a "third" beyond the dyadic relationship is explored through the work of Green. Finally I turn to the place of affect, rather neglected by psychoana-

---

[1]Van Haute (2002) gives an interesting summary of some of these formulations, which are scattered throughout Lacan's writings. Classical analysis has been guilty of similar attempts to find a common structure or etiology for classes of patients, which suggests a temptation to make the discipline "scientific."

lytic theory, and attempt to show its symbolic function, as an extension of a Lacanian model.

THE MIRROR STAGE

One place where Lacan did use biologic references was around the structuring effect of the visual gestalt, for example, on imprinting or mating behavior in birds. An animal is sensitive to a particular configuration of shapes or colors that sets off an automatic response, a neurobiological function virtually absent in humans. Of course there must be preprogrammed sequences in early life, but Lacan generally regarded these as fundamentally irrelevant for psychoanalysis, which is interested in a human subject who arises not out of a biological program but from contact with other subjects and from a cultural system that structures this contact. Yet, in the case of the mirror phase, Lacan (1949) proposed what seems like an inborn developmental stage. Following the observations of infant researchers of his time, he noted the excitement of the 18-month-old infant who identifies with his own visual gestalt in the mirror and hypothesized that this experience of wholeness forms the foundations of the ego. Even in this example, the infant seems already to have emergent psychological properties that grow out of the preceding mother–child matrix. The important point for Lacan to which we return many times was the opposition (later the complementarity) between this mirroring identification of "that is me," as an objective or concrete false self, and the symbolic framework of language, history, and society, which creates the speaking, named subject.

From a Lacanian perspective, subjectivity is an effect of language. Clearly, without the symbolic structure of differentiated signifiers, an individual identity would scarcely be possible. We depend on a proper name and a constellation of abstract terms to locate ourselves in the human world, and we must navigate through language to satisfy our drives and desires. On the other hand, this preeminence of language, of the signifier, without question conveys an abstract and austere conception of human beings that has been repugnant to many readers. The seeming absence of affect in this theorization stands out as a major deficiency of Lacan's work.

Of course, it is often said that in Freudian terminology word representations carry the energies that will structure our conscious experience, including those affective expressions central to our subjective coherence and continuity through time. From this perspective, we could say that affect always follows meaning—what moves us is what holds personal significance for us—and that meaning is, therefore, an effect of the signifier. Yet affect can sometimes overwhelm meaning, just as drive expression in Freudian terms can be destructive of boundaries or limits if not modulated by containing structures. Green (1977) insisted on this point, comparing disruptive affect to "a river overflowing its bed" (p. 206). For Freud, affect was the conscious expression of bodily sources of excitation linked with word representations that permit an emotional state to be consciously known and communicated with others. Proper control and "binding" of excitation, as we know, was considered by Freud to be a basic function of the psychic apparatus.

This brief sketch of a Freudian model serves to alert us to some difficulties in understanding the dilemmas of the speaking subject. If affect is important, how can it be integrated with the powerful notion of symbolic systems that seem transbiological (in the sense that culture stands beyond biology)? Is affect inborn like the gestalts to which Lacan referred and to which Pinker (2002), for instance, seems to be alluding from his evolutionary perspective? Does this conception have anything at all to do, as Freud believed, with the notion of aggressive and sexual drives? Or, could affects themselves be considered cultural products? There is an important difference between a limited number of inherited expressive facial configurations and the experience and understanding of affect (see Stern, 1985, pp. 64–68). In this regard, infant researchers infer mediating functions in the mind through which physiologic reactions become subjectivized and translated into communicable experience. As I develop in chapter 3, I regard Freud's construct of the ego ideal as describing this function, specifically by internalization of transgenerational cultural models providing the imagery, metaphors, and narratives through which emotion can be intelligibly or permissibly expressed.

In any event, it does seem a relatively common clinical finding that many severely damaged or traumatized patients appear to be trapped between powerful emotional urges and the seeming impossibility of their expression or satisfaction. This type of impasse seems to be characteristic in particular of many of those patients who describe something lacking in their existence—the paradoxical feeling of "not being in life," of not existing nor feeling real as embodied, vital beings. They may complain of having no feelings or, conversely, of a panoply of disconnected and senseless emotions that leave them rudderless on an unending turbulence. I include in such cases, among numerous possible examples, Mitchell's (1991) description of "problems of self-definition" of a "postmodern multiplex and discontinuous self" and Bromberg's (1998) evocation of "discontinuous self-states," although their characterizations rely on a Sullivanian paradigm of relational selves, which I find incomplete. Fairbairn's (1944) portrayal of the schizoid sense of futility, elaborated by Guntrip (1971), also addressed this problem, although Fairbairn's description became bogged down in cumbersome internal object mechanics. Guntrip (1971) wrote about "the schizoid problem" concerning "the basic reality and viability of the central core of selfhood in the person" (pp. 150–151). Their wishful postulation of a pristine, "unsplit" self seems problematic to me. Kohut, as I develop, spoke of a lack of self-cohesion as the central deficit in narcissistic patients, but may have conceived of the notion of a "superordinate self" in a too-literal way, perhaps embracing the familiar ideology of an "American way of life" of wholeness, initiative, and mastery. Eigen (1981) most closely approaches my position in this chapter with his powerful interpretation of "faith" as the central concern of Winnicott, Lacan, and Bion in the subject's struggle to be. He wrote, "for Winnicott, the essential battle is over one's sense of realness: does one feel real to oneself or merely a phantom or splinter self?" (p. 425).

KOHUT: THE COHESIVE SELF AND ITS AVATARS

Among other modern theorists, perhaps Heinz Kohut (1977) came closest to grappling with the kinds of clinical problems presented by patients for whom, as Little (1985) wrote, "anxieties concerning existence, survival, or identity predominate" (p. 15). Through his notion of the cohesive self, Kohut provided a way of understanding the intuitively familiar but hard to grasp qualities of "centeredness," "having it together," and emotional availability which are often notable by their absence in narcissistically damaged patients and address basic issues of agency, relatedness to others, and subjective vitality too often neglected by ego psychologists. Moreover, in the concept of the selfobject, he recognized the importance of abandoning the model of an encapsulated subject as pure interiority and recognized the necessary role of others in sustaining the self. These features of Kohut's work offer bridges to Lacan, a connection examined by Muller (1989), who has drawn attention to their shared critique of ego psychology and the importance for both thinkers of mirroring phenomena and, in different ways, of desire as a measure of authenticity in the subject. In the following section, I take the position of assuming a common clinical object that both thinkers attempted to describe through different vocabularies. I hope to show why we need to read Lacan to go beyond Kohut, but also how Kohut helps us to rethink Lacanian principles.

In many ways, what Kohut called the cohesive self is best known through its failures or absence, which he addressed in his analysis of narcissistic disorders. For Kohut (1977, 1987), the developing "self" is at risk of fragmentation if not supported by types of interchanges with its objects (or with selfobjects) that he called "mirroring of the self" and "targets for idealization" (p. 185). In most cases, according to him, mirroring relates to maternal acceptance of grandiose ambitions in the child, which provides a kind of container for what might otherwise be disruptive wishes, whereas idealization involves the paternal object. The content of these developmentally primitive, grandiose ambitions is unclear but seemed for Kohut, as I read him, to have mainly to do with narcissistic fantasies of omnipotence and with exhibitionistic needs. Perhaps mirroring implicitly entails a necessary sustaining of illusions or of transitional realities, as Winnicott theorized, a necessary step in the development of an infant's sense of aliveness and spontaneity. The sexual or drive aspects of "ambition," still following Kohut, are secondary to lack of selfobject response as "disintegration products." Idealization or idealizing selfobject relations, on the other hand, involve principally a transfer of infantile narcissism onto (usually) the father, which creates what he termed a "pole of ideals" toward which the self can strive and, in this respect at least, appears closely related to the functions of the ego ideal. From these assumptions or hypotheses flows Kohut's (1977) formulation of the "tension arc" between the two poles of ambition and ideals as the basis for what he termed the bipolar self—a self "driven by ambitions and led by ideals" (p. 180).

There seems to be widespread agreement that the phenomena reported by Kohut are common in the treatment of narcissistically damaged patients, who, he would say, have not established a firmly cohesive nuclear self. These persons have lacked the requisite selfobject experiences and have thereby been obliged to resort to defensive measures to protect themselves against the threat of disintegration anxieties, a fundamental experience for those lacking a secure sense of personal existence. Moreover, Kohut's concept of a tension arc contributes a powerful dynamic metaphor for the process that sustains the sense of having a life. I conceive of the tension arc as an ongoing flow of personal desires toward a tolerable and communicable means of expression that stabilizes or shapes the experience of aliveness. In terms of theory, however, we could question whether Kohut's narrow and vague definition of ambitions is a reduction of a richer psychoanalytic understanding and whether the model of paternal idealization is adequate to address the phenomenology of the ego ideal (not explicitly discussed by him). It is also puzzling that Kohut did not refer to Winnicott, whose notion of the true and false self echoed a long tradition of concern about authenticity in the Western philosophical tradition. Finally, although Kohut's notion of the self has proven useful in analytic practice (he without a doubt was responsible for the attention devoted to the self in North America), it carries a certain false concreteness, as though referring to an entity of some kind (a conception that has its defenders, of course).

In place of Kohut's concept of a cohesive self, suggesting a firmly established homuncular nucleus, with misleading connotations of wholeness and "presence" (Derrida, 1974) or of an essential unity (Khan, 1974),[2] it may be useful to think in terms of a project of subjective coherence and selfhood. Self might be better considered as an emergent but ill-defined shape, perhaps closer to the Lacanian

---

[2]Derrida's (1974) work of postmodern deconstruction was a study of how certain metaphors or ideologies become enshrined in the way language is used and thereby perpetuate illusions—like the "full presence" of a discrete subject. He felt that Lacan was vulnerable to the same criticisms, although remaining quite affirmative about Lacan's overall project. Khan (1974) was, if anything, a disciple of Winnicott's in the British society, but who yet raised questions around how the "true self" was conceptualized.

metaphor of a chain of sustainable discourse through which desire
as a free flow of affect can insist. The self has to be told or narrated,
as Schafer (1992) has recently insisted, reminding us that there is
no "entity" of self existing apart from the discourse that conveys
it. Narrations about the self, of course, are subject to the effects of
desires and defenses against it, and to all the contradictory demands and pressures of subjective existence, which make any kind
of substantial coherence a mythic or idealized belief. Of course,
the concept of desire as used by Lacan is not identical with affective expression. No doubt that affect can disguise desire or misdi-
rect it. Yet it seems hard to imagine the vitality of desire as a unique
human process animating a state of aliveness without interweaving
it with the pulse of emotional arousal that is an inextricable element in every communication. In referring to a sustainable discourse, I employ Lacan's shorthand term for the very complex
process of ongoing symbolization and construction that his difficult notion of "full speech" suggests. In full speech, according to
Lacan, the subject can come closer to his desire, which above all is
to achieve recognition from the other. This conception retains the
dynamic structure of Kohut's tension arc, continuously translating
desires (we need to develop this concept, as well) "upward" to a
more elaborated level of symbolic expression.

  In contrast to what might be termed "a well-functioning tension
arc," analytic practitioners are familiar with the desubjectifying,
disorganizing effect of powerful emotions that sometimes seem to
follow a course of their own, as if under the sway of a repetition
compulsion, restaging an emotional scenario that seems outside of
chronological time. In such cases, in lieu of remembering, the patient
enacts a massive transference repetition, collapsing past and present
so that space for thought or "making sense" is unavailable. Without
the therapeutic alliance Freud (1920) described in "Beyond the Pleasure Principle," in which the analysand retains "some degree of
aloofness" (p. 19) and capacity for self-observation, pure reliving
of traumatic experience is usually disasterous for analytic work.
Affective discharge that is not contained by a structure merely repeats a traumatic situation from the past in a slightly altered form,
which only leads to greater subjective disorganization and fragmentation of self-experience. In the worst case, when there is no
analytic space in which to talk about such episodes, treatment comes
to a premature end via a suicide attempt or hospitalization.

In his early work, Lacan (1953, 1953–1954), like Kohut, was responding to the neglect of the human subject by what he viewed as the mechanistic excesses of ego psychology. He turned to a rich philosophical tradition to find some support for a psychoanalytic theory outside the natural sciences beloved of Freud. In this quest, he was notably influenced by Heidegger's notions of authenticity in his conception of full and empty speech. In full speech, desire apparently flows or "insists" along the chain of signifiers animating the subject (Lacan, 1972–1973), whereas in empty speech we hear the effects of what Loewald (1980) was to call "a lifeless nimbleness" (p. 190), an agile display of representations devoid of affect. Khan (in Winnicott, 1986), elaborating on Winnicott's equation of boredom in the listener with psychopathology, referred to "an interminable verbiage" that petrifies narrative. Khan wrote, "the patient who compels boring narrative on us is not letting language and metaphor elaborate or change his experience" (p. 3). Empty speech presents what Lacan labeled "the wall of words" in his famous schema L, a flow of defensive and closed talk that maintains an imaginary (illusory) sense of self. This seems extremely close to Khan's formulations and to Eigen's (1981) work, which explicitly addressed the issue of authenticity. Lacan sought at this point in his theorizing to find a way around this wall, so that communication could become open to the "otherness" of desire and to the symbolic sources of subjectivity that had been repressed or barred. In fact, seeing the problem of empty speech, perhaps as did Heidegger, as a widespread symptom of the alienation of modern man, he imagined that psychoanalysis might offer a broader help to society than a simple treatment of individual neuroses.

As I have suggested, probably Kohut and Lacan were responding to the relative neglect of the issues of subjectivity, selfhood, and authenticity in classical ego psychology. By proposing the ego of the structural model in place of concepts like self or subject, which it may have mistrusted as excessively philosophical and unscientific, ego psychology lent itself to a mechanistic approach. The ego, in this conception, uses its innate synthesizing capacity to mediate between the different psychic agencies, which are its masters, by constructing an ever-changing kaleidoscope of self and object representations, continuously equilibrating the tensions within the system. From the perspective of agency, this ego functions essentially like the virtual subject of artificial intelligence,

which is to say like no subject at all!³ At best, by positing mechanisms of secondary autonomy resulting from the interaction of
drives with an average expectable environment, ego psychology
offered an ethology or psychobiology of adaptation, rather than a
"tension arc" of existential uncertainty and risk.

Lacan and, in different terms, Kohut, believed that a narcissistic
object relationship—a recourse to the mirror as a defining structure
of the self—was a response to the threat of fragmentation. That is,
in the face of a threatening encounter with another, unknown subject that could overwhelm the capacity of the individual to symbolize
and contain subjective experience (his affects, desires, fantasies),
he or she seeks support for a failing sense of cohesion by restricting
the other to the function of a mirror. Here, Lacan was greatly influenced by the philosopher Kojeve's lectures on Hegel, which he attended during his analytic training years.⁴ The encounter with the
other as another subject, as portrayed in Hegel's famous parable
of the master and the slave, threatens the defensive, narcissistic
organization of self by the inevitability of being seen and redefined
through an unfamilar gaze. Solomon (1983) presented the apt illustration of a solitary hiker contemplating an inspiring view who
is suddenly interrupted by the presence of another person. Suddenly his experience is disrupted and changed. In Lacan's (1949)
conception of the mirror relation, the subject attempts to assimilate
the other to a familiar internal schema of self and object images in
order to master the threat of the unknown other. In the imaginary
(mirror) relationship, the object will function as a confirmation of
the desired self-definition of the subject (or, conversely, he will identify with the imago of the object). From this narcissistic position,
the subject attempts to project (or to assume) a preferred image of
wholeness, which will be validated by its reflection in the other.
The other (another person, another subject, the analyst) then becomes the means to enact either a reflected confirmation of an
ideal self or the reciprocal role that self demands. In Kohut's terms,
the other becomes a pure selfobject, propping up a weakly cohe-

---

³I have discussed some of these variant conceptions of self and self-representation
  in my paper, "The Concept of the Self in Psychoanalytic Theory and Its
  Philosophical Foundations" (Kirshner, 1991).
⁴The Hegel-Kojeve influence has been addressed by many authors. See, for
  example, Van Haute (2002), Borch-Jacobsen (1990), and Ver Eecke (1983).

sive self. Lacan called this type of relationship "specular" or imaginary, unrelated to the structural and symbolic realities that define the subject and alienate her from her desire by reinforcing an ego whose function is to distort reality and to obscure desire. Who one is, authentically, in "full speech," is not who one appears to be or tries to impress others as being, and the latter "inauthentic self," as we know from extremely narcissistic patients, can manifest itself in either positive (grandiose) or negative (self-critical) forms. In what follows, I present two pared-down case vignettes to illustrate these mirroring concepts.

TWO EXAMPLES OF MIRRORING TRANSFERENCES

Mr. Small described a life-long feeling about himself that he was empty and unworthy. His mother had criticized him as too slow and an academic mediocrity, despite his fairly good scholastic record. He believed that he never did anything well enough and saw this as an intrinsic personality characteristic, an attitude that colored most of his life experience. In his analysis, Mr. Small insisted on his deficiency and believed that he was probably incapable of becoming a good patient who could meet his analyst's requirements. When the analyst (whom I supervised) attempted to encourage Mr. Small to say his own thoughts and feelings instead of striving to meet some imagined standard of performance, he felt admonished for being unoriginal and "coming up short." The analyst's subsequent line of interpretation that Mr. Small carried a fantasy of inadequacy dominating all his relationships was likewise taken as a criticism. He associated these and other interventions to his mother's well-meaning efforts to improve him, which seemed to reinforce his assumption that the analyst knew what he should be saying and doing in the sessions. Here, the analyst seemed stuck in a reciprocal interaction pattern that "mirrored" the patient's self-image. The fantasy of being objectified as defective in mother's eyes sustained Mr. Small's conscious ego identity, while unconsciously, no doubt, involved him in a particular kind of satisfaction in relation to her (in the dual relation characteristic of the mirror). The analyst was participating unwittingly in various ways in an old pattern (a relationship in which the subject was criticized as not good enough), which, at this point in the treatment, was reenacted and not able to be understood. Fortunately, she came to recognize her refusal of his transference projection of a perfectionistic (m)other and began to respond more sensitively to Mr. Small's fantasy of another maternal rejection.

Mr. Grand came to analysis because of his failure to sustain close relationships with his partners, in whom he always lost interest. Friends told him he was too critical and self-centered in these affairs. Although he did express a high opinion of his talents and accomplishments, he sensed a difficulty in making emotional connections, which he characterized as having been cool or even nonexistent in his family. His parents, in fact, despite his enormous early promise and the fine education and training they had supported, seemed unappreciative of his accomplishments. Initially, he viewed his analyst as a master in the area of human relationships who could show him the royal road to full self-realization and success. Holding an elevated notion of her importance in their community, based on a superlative recommendation by a former classmate, he hoped to learn the secret of her greatness. Unfortunately, these positive anticipations soon ran into feelings that the analyst was not taking him seriously enough and was withholding the direction and advice he needed to progress. This opened the way to some productive exploration of his disappointing relationship with his mother, where the analyst's empathy was reassuring. Unfortunately, he seemed to hear this as confirmation that his mother had withheld something that the analyst could now provide. When he began to press her more and more impatiently to provide these "answers," the atmosphere of the sessions turned more tense. The analyst continued without much success to encourage Mr. Grand to explore his own thoughts, a move he regarded with some validity as an evasive technique. In a moment of exasperation, the analyst observed that he was assuming a knowledge on her part that did not exist, something that could only be worked out by him alone. Eventually she disclosed that she truly did not have the answers he sought. In his frustration, Mr. Grand now began to attack the analyst and the process of treatment itself. After a vacation break, he decided not to return.

With Mr. Grand, the analyst seemed to be doing well in exploring what he had attempted to secure from his unresponsive mother. She did not see the repetition of his powerful idealization of a perfect mother in whose eyes he sought unsuccessfully to be lovable. With the intensification of his unrealistic demands, the analyst retreated to the position of "a real object" from her idealized transference role, which Lacan called the "subject supposed to know" or the "supposed subject of knowledge." According to Lacan, it is this basic transference that elicits a patient's demands and incites a desire that had been repressed. In this case, the analyst's appeal to Mr. Grand's observing ego and a nonexistent therapeutic alliance led to a reversal of the mirror, with the patient now moving into the position of the ideal ego (the imago of the mother), while his analyst was left to represent his devalued self.

Mr. Small and Mr. Grand illustrate the reciprocal relationship characterizing the mirror transference in which the fantasy of a perfect self is at stake for a narcissistically fragile subject. These men sought confirmation of their ideal egos from their analysts, who initially tried to disentangle themselves from the transference position. Mr. Small was encouraged to express his own ideas, whereas Mr. Grand was asked to renounce his unrealistic demands. As we have observed, the dual relationship can vary in tone, depending on the locus of the identification (ego merged with ideal self or facing an idealized object), and can easily be reversed. Thus Mr. Grand could feel either inadequate and small or superior and inflated in the regard of his therapist, depending on which position in the relationship he had assumed. The important thing is the rigidity of the dyadic mode replayed in the here and now, shutting off access to a dynamic and painful personal history, including disappointments and crucial failures of empathic response by important others. For Lacan (1953–1954), if the therapist does not abandon her position as the supposed subject of knowledge (thus representing the Other in the patient's transference), she will uncover the history behind the frozen images of the mirror and, eventually, destabilize this imaginary relation. As we will see, Lacan's conception of therapeutic action at the time revolved around the restoration of the deficient ego ideal and symbolic identification. Mr. Grand's therapist slipped from this position by attempting a "real" relationship (real, of course, only in terms of her needs for a reasonable ally, not necessarily the patient's), which may have left him feeling abandoned and needing to defensively devalue her. We might say that her gift of a caring relationship and offer to identify with her more reasonable ego failed. Had he remained in treatment (the accident of the vacation might have been fatal here), they might have been able to explore this enactment, which was clearly related to the problem for which he had originally sought treatment.

All therapists are tempted from time to time to appeal to the "observing ego," to educate, or to cajole the patient into giving up unrealistic transference expectations and taking responsibility for working together to solve a problem. To state this another way, there is an inevitable oscillation between the analyst's transference position as "subject of knowledge" (the Other who knows the meaning of the patient's symptoms) and her "irreducible subjectivity." When the analyst's subjective response grows out of her own needs or discomfort, it can break the mirror and, as in Mr. Grand's case, lead to a reversal of imagos (a projective identification) that can be hard to interpret or undo. Many times, however, this misattunement can be acknowledged and explored, like any empathic failure, with considerable therapeutic benefit. Conversely, simply remaining within the mirror relationship can perpetuate an endless narcissistic longing that blocks insight and memory. There seems to be the following paradox in the Lacanian theory of the therapeutic mirror: Mirroring creates a transferential tension that must be sustained for deeper developments to take place, but, as an end in itself, it can only stalemate this process.

The Lacanian position relies heavily on an interpretation of mirroring as misrecognition and distortion, supporting an imaginary ego that systematically falsifies reality in order to sustain a narcissistic illusion of wholeness. In Lacan's early writings, he saw mirroring as a trap for both analyst and patient, which had to be subverted by the speaking relationship (in opposition to the specular, fantasy one). Later, the imaginary dimension was accorded more value in the construction of subjective experience, as a link to the "real" that underpins it (Julien, 1985). Reading Lacan through Kohut, as it were, mirroring can also be understood more benignly as part of the normal process of empathy, when the analyst attunes as best he or she can to the patient's demand for recognition. This demand, for Kohut (1987), represents the need for repair of a vulnerable or weakened self by a selfobject function that failed to be supplied at a crucial developmental time (this dynamic seems applicable to both Mr. Small and Mr. Grand, who both failed to elicit the admiring sparkle in the mother's eye that Kohut emphasized). We might define this use of empathy in its best connotation as an attempt to offer accurate recognition, as opposed to Lacans's harsh diagnosis of participation in a narcissistic fantasy. This distinction corresponds in some respects to Winnicott's (1954) separation of needs from wishes, in which, he proposed, need grows out of a regression to the point of failure of a necessary environmental provision. Thus, to oversimplify, Mr. Small was not appreciated nor loved for himself by his mother, whereas Mr. Grand was resentfully an instrument of his parents' narcissistic wishes. A developmental need was not satisfied during a crucial period, and the gap was covered over with a defensive ego organization analogous to a false self. In this sense, the selfobject may supply a real need in the transference, albeit a symbolic (not a literal replacement) version of the missing element.

Kohut's concept of the selfobject, as we know, describes an object who is not truly other, nor yet a simple constituent of the self, but functions as a kind of transitional object, mixing up self and other in a way that should not be sorted out. Given the fragility of the human psyche, Kohut argued, the availability of selfobjects is a universal requirement for subjective coherence, analogous to the Winnicottian concept of a necessary zone of illusion in all human experience. Like Winnicott's transitional object, the source or nature of the selfobject must not be questioned to be effective. Similarly, the selfobject is not real but is a construction in the intermediate space between subject and object, with contributions from both sides. It is thereby imaginary (Lacan) and illusory (Winnicott), although these terms do not capture the quality of the mutual construction involved in which the subject's inchoate need encounters a symbolically prepared other. In this sense, the analyst's empathic response does not necessarily or exclusively involve compliance with narcissistic wishes but can be seen as a kind of performative communication offering a point of contact with a structured social order. That is, the analyst's words do not simply gratify the patient but enact a form of social recognition of something that was lacking in his early experience and to which he was entitled. Lacan would not have used the term, need, for this type of situation, although it seems to me legitimate to speak in Lacanian terms of the child's need for a parent to assume a symbolic function. He did speak about a so-called *point de capiton* (anchoring point, as in upholstery buttons), quilting the impersonal flow of words to a reference point established in the symbolic order. This metaphor represents a halt to the endless sliding of the signifier, binding the speaking subject to particular signifieds—links to a web of social meanings shared by individual subjects that enables communication to take place.[5] Perhaps we could speak of an empathic *point de capiton,* in which a specific intersubjective interaction links the subject to a symbolic other. Kohut's work showed that in specific instances of self pathology (the threat of fragmentation, for example), the immediate requirement for the analyst is to accept the role of selfobject and not to attempt interpretation prematurely (there is no possibility of Freud's "aloofness" on either side).

On the other hand, the universal need for selfobjects and the inevitable recourse to the mirror relation both in normal subjects and, as a desperate quest for repair or completion, in patients suffering from a damaged self, exemplifies the very difficulty of sustaining a position as subject, which is the theme of this chapter. Based on fantasies of reciprocal identity and implicit understanding, the dyadic mirror solution leaves the subject extremely vulnerable to the other, who can enslave or exploit him (by manipulating the dependent selfobject transference), and exposes him to risk of the inauthenticity of a false self (by identification of the patient with a partial or distorted image). In the latter case, it could function as the relational equivalent of the "wall of words" referred to by Lacan as a major impediment to treatment, preventing the analyst from finding any freedom to express him or herself or to open a dialogue about anything outside the selfobject relationship, thereby stalemating the analytic process by confining it to a narrow band of experiences already familiar to the patient. It may well be that the contemporary interest in analysts' self-disclosure is a response to this type of impasse, attempting to destabilize a rigid mirror transference by introducing more of the analyst's subjectivity directly into the relationship. As we saw, this was what Mr. Grand's analyst attempted. Lacan, in response to this problem, referred to the possibility for triangulation within the analytic dialogue as a means of getting around the wall and engaging less conscious and narcissistically invested imagos of the patient. He observed that

---

[5]The *point de capiton* was discussed by Wilden (1968) and Van Haute (2002). It was mentioned by Lacan (1955–1956) in his seminar on the psychoses in which he proposed that a minimum number of such quiltings of signifer to signified is required to enable a personal (nonpsychotic) discourse (p. 269).

when the analyst interprets, he or she does so from another place than the position the patient anticipates and addresses issues differently from what was expected within the mirror transference. Although cast by Lacan in structural terms, his formulation seems close to the classic Freudian conception of transference interpretation. That is, by interpreting (commenting, clarifying, etc.), the analyst indicates an interest in something a bit outside the conscious field of the patient and addresses less conscious aspects of his or her psychic functioning. Along these same lines, one could say that any interpretation that departs from the most attuned empathic mirroring mode will inevitably reveal something of the subjectivity of the analyst. This expression of the analyst's subjectivity (choosing to respond at a particular time and in a particular way to the patient) undermines the imaginary transference and opens the door toward a different kind of interaction.

THE SYMBOLIC DIMENSION, KOHUT TO GREEN

Although his earliest work (1949) focused on the importance of the mirror stage and problems of identification with an image, Lacan soon began to emphasize the symbolic relationship that destabilizes this structure. His major explanatory tool came from his conception of the symbolic order derived from the anthropological structuralism of Lévi-Strauss and the linguistic theory of Saussure, which he believed addressed the basic level of psychoanalytic intervention implicit in Freud's writings. In this model, the therapeutic action of psychoanalysis depends principally on a rectification of the mirror relationship, by replacing the aim of completion of a narcissistic image (which he equated with the American technical principle of strengthening the patient's ego by identification with the analyst, see Lacan, 1958) with a recognition of the patient's own desire within his unique historical, autobiographic context. In the analytic setting, the subject's words disrupt his anchoring to a stable image, revealing a succession of identifications—parts of a history that was not historicized and thus not available in the mirror. The well-known designation of Lacan's "return to Freud" was a product of his shift in interest toward the functions of speech and the field of language (the theme of his Rome conference of 1953), which he believed were being ignored by the current generation of ego psychologists ("a technique is being handed on in a cheerless manner . . . a formalism pushed to . . . ceremonial lengths" [p. 37]). Whether this shift was necessitated by limitations in clinical practice and or by Lacan's reading of structuralist thinkers (the climate of post-war French thought), it led to a major reinterpretation of subjectivity, which now was seen as structural (the effect of structures extrinsic to the individual person) and linguistic (dependant on language). In place of his previous emphasis on imagos like the ideal ego or any other fantasy self-representation, a symbolic order consisting of kinship and status systems, structures of age and gender, and rules of inheritance and succession, operating by a kind of secondary process logic, became the principal determinant of individual identity, and the gestaltic identification as a whole self in the imaginary register of the mirror was seen as a treacherous lure. The analyst was admonished not to think in terms of object relations, which for Lacan consisted of imaginary constructions, but, rather, to pay attention to the patient's words, to the text, not to the psychology of the author. In the treatment situation, the structuring effect of a "third" was now proposed as the crucial element, creating an analytic space in which symbolic meanings could be explored and elaborated.

The concept of the third was developed by French authors influenced by Lacan but had its roots in Freud's emphasis on the structuring effects of the triangular situation of the oedipal phase (Kirshner, 1991). Green (1975) has consistently advanced this perspective, which could be summarized succinctly by stating that the analyst is not exclusively a selfobject or mirror for the patient, but is crucially a new or unknown object speaking from a different place from where the patient expects. That is, the triadic position is fundamentally inherent in the structure of analysis in the sense that it is impossible to remain exclusively within a selfobject mode and not to speak as a separate subject. As we commented, the analyst inevitably addresses the patient's unconscious from this position, as well as implicitly offering an expression of his own unconscious by choice of tone and words and timing of intervention. The patient responds to these analytic symbolizations with a new set of signifiers (of associations). The invisible and rapid verbal interaction of analyst and patient creates a new entity beyond the conscious experience of either participant but one which belongs in some sense to both. As the French psychoanalyst Serge

Viderman (1979) wrote in an influential paper, interpretive speech provides a representation for archaic experiences "in a form that exists nowhere in the unconscious of the patient or anywhere else but in the analytic space that provides it with form" (p. 262). Ogden (1994) explored this theme in the English language literature, emphazing the co-construction of the analytic third.

From this perspective, the expression of the analysand's unconscious is linked inseparably with the analyst's function, which depends on the mobilization of his or her own unconscious. The offer of analysis immediately evokes a transference in susceptible subjects who are attracted by the fantasy of "the supposed subject of knowledge," the one who in fantasy holds the secrets of their unconscious desires. The analysand's speech represents an amalgam of signifiers carrying unconscious meanings unknown to her but that will be interpreted or simply responded to, explicitly or implicitly, by the analyst. That response then calls upon further associations from the patient and so on, creating over time a unique conceptual and metonymic structure that belongs to the two participants. This process has been discussed by Green (1975) in relation to the work of Bion for whom the analyst supplies first a container for the patient's content and then a content for the patient's container (via a "metabolized" interpretation). Green's formulation seems to me quite close to Lacan's (1953) well-known statements that the unconscious is "the discourse of the Other" (p. 55) and that "the Other is the locus in which is constituted the I of speech" (1955, p. 41). In essence, both assertions mean that the speech of the subject associating in analysis is determined by structures outside of consciousness—by the field of the Other, the network of linguistic and cultural rules that provides the ground for a subject who will emerge in varying shapes and at different moments as figure. In the transference, the analyst occupies the place of the Other, containing the speech that this arrangement evokes, then continuously interpreting it back to the analysand (providing a new content to be contained). The Other is another way of naming the symbolic order. Of course, the rules of this order (of the cultural matrix) have been learned within a specific familial context, unique to the person, hence conferring an individual and more or less coherent character to each subject. However, there is always inconsistency and ambiguity in these internalized messages from the Other (the mother in the first instance) for each

person, so that identity is not fixed. Against this fluidity, according
to Lacan, the subject organizes a stable ego, which is based initially, as we have seen, on the identifications of the mirror stage.
To summarize: like all relationships, the analytic situation is based
to some degree on a kind of primary mirroring or dyadic selfobject
arrangement, but it also holds the power to destabilize the ego and
its customary modes of interaction by opening an analytic potential space, which permits the play of intersubjective exchanges.
Viderman (1979) underlined the importance of affective communication in this process which "is only possible in a specific
environment . . . in which the affects and counteraffects of the two
organizers of analytic space interact" (p. 282).

Perhaps because of intuitions similar to those of Lacan re-
garding the limits of selfobject relationships, Kohut postulated the
"pole of ideals" at one end of the tension arc of his bipolar self.
This innovation suggests that the self is not simply hungry for mirroring but requires a set of values or structuring principles external to it to give a shape to its desires. This aspect is made clear in
Ornstein's (1980) presentation of the theory of the bipolar self,
which emphasizes internalization and structure building. Although
Kohut spoke of the pole of ideals in classic Freudian terms as a
residue of infantile narcissism via idealization of the parents (an
interpretation that from a Lacanian perspective would seem to place
it within the imaginary order—as the product of a fantasy), it is
equally true that ideals derive from cultural symbolism, which
stands as a "third" position beyond the needy, exhibitionistic self
and its objects and shapes them. Wolf (1980), speaking of the development of the self, wrote, "as long as a person is securely embedded in a social matrix that provides him with a field in which he
can find the needed mirroring responses and the availability of
idealizable values, he will feel comfortably affirmed in his total
self" (p. 128). Although not explicitly spelled out in Kohut's theory,
it seems to me that the self psychologists' distinction between narcissistic grandiosity and idealization of social values (or their rep-
resentatives) roughly parallels the differentiation Lacan attempted
to make between Freud's notions of the ideal ego and the ego ideal.[6]

---

[6]Very few commentators accept Lacan's reading of Freud on this point (see
Diatkine, 2000), which depends on only a few early references. Probably, Lacan
himself must take credit for this construction.

For Lacan, the ideal ego refers to a grandiose fantasy of the self, whereas the ego ideal derives from an internalization of the symbolic order that bounds and locates the subject.

Freud (1914) observed that people strive to be their own ideal, with a persisting wish for omnipotence, against an ideal imposed from without. Whatever Freud may have had in mind precisely, Lacan wanted to contrast the fantasies of a grandiose ego denying limitations (the ideal ego) with an ego structured by the principle of differentiation within a symbolic system (the ego ideal). Symbolic systems by their nature involve relationships of difference and separateness between their various elements. These qualities were connected by Lacan with the paternal principle of differentiation from the mother, because fatherhood exemplifies a "third" element, a symbolic role, which destabilizes the imaginary oneness of the dyad. What he called symbolic castration involves renunciation of primary process fantasies of oneness and fusion with the mother and of the fantasy of wholeness that accompanies them. These fantasies, which belong to the imaginary register, are corrected by the limiting conditions of a symbolic order based on separateness and finitude. Freud (1914) said that these conditions have a social aspect, as the shared ideals of a family, class, or nation. Here, I believe, one can attempt a rapprochement of Kohut with Lacan. They each saw the human subject as the product of a structure (tension arc to pole of ideals, the symbolic order) outside of conscious experience, although the notions of a third and of the triadic dimension were only minimally developed by Kohut. Because the agency of the ego ideal for Freud arises both from intrapsychic and social sources (infantile narcissism and the parents' transmission of ideals), its function may be to mediate the tensions arising within what Kohut called the bipolar structure of ambitions and ideals. Stated differently, the development of the Kohutian self requires a linkage of private embodied experiences and desires with a structuring social system that sets parameters for the subject.

Attachment to a symbolic framework through the functions of the ego ideal creates meaning and value for individuals and defines a position in the human (cultural) world which is the true bulwark against fragmentation, even in the face of traumatic experience, but it seems hard to achieve for many people. Hence the constant need for recourse to an imaginary selfobject and to the mirror function in relationships to stabilize a vacillating self, especially in modern societies where symbolic roles are much less clearly defined. A recent book by Kilborne (2002), which deals with "invisible people," elaborates the overriding importance of personal appearance and being seen in contemporary ideology. The aim is to create an image that will give a semblance of substance to the self. The counterpart for many is a self-protective fantasy of invisibility, of not being seen or known by the other. Unfortunately, Kilborne (2002) noted, such fantasies can backfire, "since they tend to produce fears of disappearing in reality" (p. 46). Investment in an image that must be strenuously defended against all threats is characteristic of patients labeled narcissistic personalities, but this pathology seems pandemic in contemporary society.

In practice, of course, symbolic attachments and imaginary mirroring are intertwined as inextricable aspects of experience, just as Winnicottian transitional relatedness and the intermediate realm of illusion pervade human life without undermining the distinction between normality and psychosis (while, of course, relativizing this difference). Against Lacan's model, as I have suggested, one could argue that the empathic gesture that responds to a patient's demand partakes of the symbolic role incarnated by the analyst, as it is the gesture of another separate subject. Without such a response, as Ferenczi (1933) argued, the treatment risks retraumatizing the patient. Only when the analyst colludes in a narcissistic fantasy to deny frustration, loss, and difference out of her or his own wishes for omnipotence or control is the symbolic function breached, usually with bad consequences.

Perhaps we could propose that ideals (in Kohut's conception) derive from the symbolic order (Lacan's conception) of which they represent an internalized element. Tolpin (1980) referred to the "elevated powerful world" (p. 305) of the idealized selfobjects, offering the example of an admired teacher on the podium nodding to his rapt pupils. Apart from its resemblance to the relationship of Kohut's followers to the master himself, the setup described (teacher, school, auditorium) is essentially a symbolic one, despite the magical or imaginary connotations of the specular "nod." In my view, the self psychologists regularly blur these two functions— no doubt always intertwined, as I have noted—not giving full due to the symbolic Other behind the selfobject (the object in Winnicottian terms that survives all the mirror fantasies of incorporation and projection by the subject). There is a determining symbolic structure beyond the Kohutian self of lived experience, distinct from the imaginary projects of a grandiose self or, in Lacan's vocabulary, of an ideal ego.

In terms of object relations theory, in which one can speak, for example, of the self and the object world, self and objects are constructed mutually and come into being in the course of early development according to a basic set of organizing principles. This "basic set" has to do with the fundamental reality of differentiation and separation through the assumption of language, which Lacan described in his exegesis of the famous *fort-da*[7] game reported by Freud (1920). When the child plays this game, he is essentially representing presence and absence of the mother by alternation of two phonemes, which happen to be the German words for here and gone. The two units of sound are distinct, Lacan observed, as basic elements in the system of differentiated sounds of which a language consists. The sounds become signifiers, part of a chain of words that carries meaning, in this case a protoconcept of separation. Mother is gone, leaving the child alone to play out what has happened by use of a new linguistic expression for the preverbal experience of "awayness." Interestingly, the cognitive developmentalists Gopnik and Meltzoff (1997), in their research, pointed to the importance of this early concept in accelerating the child's intellectual development (seemingly unaware of Freud and Lacan's observations). They were interested in the construction of "theories about objects" (p. 199), extending the Piagettian perspective on the development of object constancy (physical, not human objects), noting a relation between the appearance of words like "gone" and high-level object permanence abilities. "Gone," they observed, "catches a particular contrast between ontology and phenomenology; between the fact that the world looks one way and is another way" (p. 112). Of course, the phonemes are learned (or selectively attended to) as a result of a relationship with the primordial object, the mother, already immersed in the languaged world (the subtle point made by Lacan that all her responses, whatever faint biological sources may be involved, are structured by the symbolic order).

---

[7]The *fort-da* refers to the back and forth, "here and gone" of a spool on a string thrown and recaptured by the child.

THE SYMBOLIC ORDER: WINNICOTT TO LACAN

Lacan called the entire symbolic field the Other, and he emphasized its structuring of the world into which the child is born. Modell
(1968), in speaking about the process of the child's relationship
with external reality, observed that, initially, reality is the mother,
and it is through the tie to her, through object love, that reality is
known. The term *reality* in this context carries the implications of
human or social reality, which Lacan labeled the symbolic order,
and, according to Modell, it is identified in the first instance with
the mother as the Other. Erikson's (1950) concept of basic trust
also seems to refer to more than simply trusting the mother as a
reliable person (although that may be a requirement for its establishment), but implies a confident relationship with "reality" (the
external object world) in which the child must make his or her
way. At this point in our inquiry, we need to follow Modell in
returning to Winnicott, who did understand the importance of a
symbolic space for establishment of a self. These constitute important bridges to Lacan that were elaborated by Green, as we discuss.

Winnicott's (1971) central interest was the coming to be of
the child as a separate entity with an inner world demarcated from
the object. Yet he insisted that to be sustained this private inner
world depended on a transitional space between self and objective
reality. "The use of the transitional object symbolizes the union of
two separate things, baby and mother, at a point in time and space
of the initiation of their state of separateness" (pp. 96–97). This
state of separateness depends paradoxically on the presence of the
mother, and it can be damaged, perhaps irreversibly in some cases,
by her too-long absence. In the latter situation, Winnicott (1971)
wrote, primitive defenses become mobilized in the infant to defend
against "madness," defined as the breakup of a personal continuity of existence. The process of the infant's drawing away from the
mother and forming a separate self involves the development of
internal representations within the mother–child field, in turn depending on the organization of the transitional or cultural space.
Winnicott defined the word culture as follows: "I am thinking of
something that is in the common pool of humanity, into which
individuals and groups may contribute, and from which we may
all draw *if we have somewhere to put what we find*" (p. 99). This
is close to Lacan's notion of the symbolic order, if, like his interpre-

tation of the mirror phase, a more humanized version. We put what we find into "the universal discourse" says Lacan (1954–1955, p. 283), into a network of signifiers that is a common possession of the group.

In writing of these matters, Green (1976) followed Winnicott's discussion by referring to the separation of the maternal and subjective spheres in a "state of reunion" (p. 58), which creates a potential cultural space and a feeling of coherence and consistency. The optimal intersection of these spheres produces the "affect of existence", he proposed. "This feeling of coherence and consistency—support for the pleasure in existing—is not self-evident, but must be infused by the object. The destiny of the One," Green concluded, "is to live in conjunction and/or separation from/with the Other" (p. 58; the Other referring here to the mother of infancy). That is, the fragmented incipient subject must have a relationship with the mother to achieve coherence and a sense of existing separately, a function of the maternal holding-presence. The mother becomes internalized not simply as an object but, as Green (1997) later wrote, a container or frame within which representations of objects can be created. This maternal frame (as an internalization of her holding function) might also be considered an anlage of the symbolic (some kind of protostructure in the mind), which derives from (is carried by) the child's relationship with the good object. We could develop this point by suggesting that an important function of the "good enough" mother is to foster basic trust as the basis for internalization of the symbolic order provided by the surrounding culture. To turn this point around to the perspective of the child, the ability and availability of other persons to assume symbolic roles (as mother or father, for example), which are necessary to engender a good internalized object relation, depend on an entire cultural (symbolic) system that defines, validates, and supports those roles. Erikson spoke of a cycle of generations that carries this larger holding function (a holding of the holding), which Lacan called "the big Other" (the Other). The role of mother, beyond whatever biological supports it leans on, depends on beliefs, customs, and institutions maintained by her society. Her connection to this network can be damaged at many levels, from the experience of intense physical pain to the collapse of an entire society, in which cases it falls to the mother's caretakers (or to other survivors of a disaster) to ensure repair and reestablishment of basic trust. Beyond a certain threshhold of damage, repair becomes problematic, and we then enter the territory of severe trauma and its effects.

For Green, the fundamental threats to basic trust are intrusion (excess of presence: impingement, penetration, castration) and object loss (separation, abandonment, the experientially dead mother), which become psychically organized very early in life. In his writings on this process, Green (1986) developed and clarified Lacan's and Winnicott's conceptions of the organizing function of the symbol, a process he saw as beginning with a very early triangulation between subject and object, inherently involving the father. Early triangulation is implicit in the maternal role and in speech, which structures her role, creating a space between the real of the infant–mother biological relationship and the imaginary of earliest fantasies (the Kleinian object relations of the infant, for example) within which experience can be symbolically represented.

Winnicott (1971) commented that beyond a certain limit of absence the mother is dead to the child. "This is what dead means" (p. 22), he said. In his conception of the dead mother in "La Mère Morte," Green (1980a) expanded on these few lines from *Playing and Reality*. He wrote of the unbearable separation that leads to the disinvestment of the maternal representation and thus to the psychic death of the mother (for the child). In this situation, the contents of the holding frame consist of a negative hallucination or void. By this, Green meant that the mother, even when in fact physically present, is no longer represented as a symbolic internal object. He saw the dead mother not as an object representation but as a "cold nucleus" (p. 230), one with which the subject eventually identifies. Winnicott stated that failure of the external object in some important function leads either to deadness or to a persecutory quality of the internal object, which resembles the bad object of Fairbairn (1943). Recall that Fairbairn saw neurotic guilt and so-called superego anxiety as defensive against the emergence of a primitive, destructive bad object, which attacks, as it were, the very right of the self to be. In addition to these possible outcomes, Green spoke of damage to the framing structure itself, producing disintegration anxiety.

Perhaps it is worth pausing here to reemphasize the symbolic aspects of the framing structure and of the holding and containing functions of the mother. This is an important point because it bears upon certain technical disagreements and even more fundamental conceptual ones in contemporary psychoanalysis. No doubt there has been a correct appreciation of the revolution wrought by Winnicott in bringing attention to the importance of these early functions within a psychoanalytic treatment. Green (1975) alluded to the movement in psychoanalysis away from an analysis of the content "to the analysis of the container, to the analysis of the setting itself" (p. 45). This implies a more rigorous attention to the countertransference as an inherent and necessary part of the analytic work. Certainly the emotional climate of the setting and the patient's reliance on the selfobject aspects of the relationship are now recognized as central features of any psychoanalytically informed treatment. The disagreement arises when the focus on the analyst's affective responsiveness, empathy, and openness to the patient's needs obscures or displaces the analyst's symbolic functions. Green (1999) criticized a tendency toward a kind of overprotective mothering in contemporary treatment by its emphasis on the patient's need for the analyst's availability and responsiveness, at the expense of attention to the effects of the presence of the differentiated other and to the anxieties of intrusion. For Winnicott, Green, and Lacan (of course, with important differences), the intuitive emotional response of the mother is made possible by the symbolic situation of the human family setup, which provides a space for development of a self or of a separate speaking subject. Although the analyst is not ever in precisely the same position, the maternal analogy seems to have taken firm hold, both in terms of explicitly repeating a maternal role (at times this becomes more one of a nongendered parent), and in the widely used metaphor of establishment of a relational matrix for a reconstruction of self. The important critique raised by Green is not necessarily one of overmothering, nor even of a possible overpersonalization of the analytic relationship, but rather one of neglect of the symbolizing and structuralizing functions of the mother and, by corollary, a lack of attention to these dimensions of psychoanalytic work.

As Green (1999) reiterates, returning to the Lacanian conception of a space for representation opened by a third out of the infant's immersion in the "real" of the primary object, the symbolic father (or another symbolic third) is aleady present from the very first as a major component of the psychic world of the mother. She carries "him" with her as part of the frame that holds the infant. We might say that this is a virtual space that is not able to be precisely situated in chronology (hence Green's critique of infant developmental research) but that it appears retroactively once the incipient subject can say "I." So there is an opening—an undefined zone of transitionality and "harmonious mix-up" (to use Balint's phrase)—and a language (a symbolizing structure) that fills it. To these two necessary ingredients of psychic life, Green (1999) proposed a third component incorporating the drive, the link with the body, and affect, which he criticized as missing in Lacan. His assessment of Lacan in this regard seems on the mark, especially in view of the evolution of Lacanian theory toward an almost exclusive emphasis on the signifier, in the wake of which every other human phenomenon follows. Language, Green (1973) reminded us, is empty without affect, and he has labored to develop a useful psychoanalytic theory of affect. As he would be the first to admit, however, the theory is lacking in many respects. Clearly, for a sense of vitality and existence, there must be the emotional resonance Green evokes. Yet, for affect to be bearable and vivifying, it must be to some degree expressed or expressible. It must not simply carry communicative functions (as a sign), but symbolic ones, so that a living language can inhabit the transitional space shared by the self with others.

In the preceding pages, we have traveled a difficult and circuitous route from Lacan's concepts of the imaginary order, the mirror stage, and the symbolic, through their links to Kohut's innovations involving the mirroring function of a selfobject and the bipolar self, all of these terms in some sense building on Winnicott's crucial insights about self-formation. Pursuing Modell's hypothesis abut the noncommunication of affects and Green's insistence on affect as a third constituent element of mental life, we must now turn to a closer look at the symbolic dimension of affect and its role in sustaining subjective existence.

3

The Cultural Construction of Affect

*The affect is not like a special density which would
escape an intellectual accounting. It is not to be
found in a mythical beyond of the production of the
symbol.*

—Jacques Lacan

In this chapter, I do not attempt a comprehensive review of the topic of affect, which is obviously huge and partakes of many disciplines. What I would like to explore is the perspective on affect as symbolic, that is, as culturally constructed and transmitted. In this sense, it becomes an important mediating vehicle between the private psychobiological subject and the world of other subjects in which he or she must find her place. The notion of the symbolic construction of affect emphasizes the shaping and differentiating of emotion as "signifier of the flesh" by culture, as many contemporary anthropologists insist (Levy 1973; Rosaldo, 1984; Lutz, 1988; Schweder, 1991). Emotion, wrote Lutz (1988) in an important study, is not simply a psychobiological given of human life but reflects complexly evolved systems of belief and acculturation. This was basically Lacan's point in the aforementioned quotation. Affect is not "a special density"—presumably meaning a kind of phenomenon discrete from other expressions of mental life. It is not an expression of the body independent of or beyond the symbol, but is structured like every other manifestation of human behavior and thought. For Lacan, affect cannot be separated from the unique place of desire in the constitution of the subject.

55

Of course, Lacan as usual disposed of the problem a bit too brusquely in his haste to move on to the "meat" of his presentation, which, as we know, featured the signifier as the central element of subjective experience. We should not repeat this error, as the signifier cannot be considered without emotional valence, and speech and feeling are inherently embodied. Words are constantly entangled with bodily metaphors and sensual connotations, and emotions cannot be divorced from their bodily roots. There is certainly something affectively charged about the signifier in general (there is no speech without an accompanying affect and a set of messages about how to feel about what is being said), and affect, although captured in the net of symbolic meanings, remains a universal biological property of the human species. We know, for instance, that similar situations elicit common emotional responses and that certain facial and bodily gestures are indicative of those responses across the great majority of the world's cultures. Probably these linkages are greatest in early childhood, again suggesting a "hard-wired" basis for some manifestations of affect. As Schweder (1991) argued, however, the polarizing debate about nature versus culture that has animated both anthropologists and psychoanalysts has never been more sterile than in dealing with the problem of affect. Although the "psychobiology" of emotional states seems undeniable, it is equally obvious that words and concepts for emotions, conceptions of appropriate contexts for affective expression, and private meanings of emotions and their implications for self and others vary widely across cultures and are shaped enormously by cultural experience.

If affects then are not simply "natural" responses of the organism to its environment nor direct manifestations of inborn drives, yet are omnipresent accompaniments of human interaction and private reflection, we need to inquire more deeply into their form and function in human experience. Psychoanalysis, as Green insisted, must grapple with the clinical problem of a painful lack of affect or of a sense of deadness in patients (notably those complaining of their nonexistence), as well as the more general, overarching question of how people are able most of the time to sustain a sense of vitality and aliveness, while going about their highly patterned routines and socially constructed roles. Schweder (1991) proposed the extended metaphor of "soul loss" as a comprehensive description of the multiple ways in which depression is manifested across different cultures. He noted that the experience of absence of a vital part, leaving the subject empty, sad, and frightened, with somatic symptoms, is a universally known condition, although explained in various ways by different societies. Analysts speak in terms of a loss of emotional investments, leaving the world a flatter, more barren place and depleting the ego of nourishment, while psychiatrists of our time refer to chemical imbalances and neurotransmitter deficits to describe a medical problem of depression.

Other cultures make reference to witchcraft or to a violation of spiritual principles to interpret the depressive loss of self. Schweder chose the term *soul* to refer to what he considered an observing inner self common to all peoples and societies—a piece of the human endowment, as it were—a self that can lose its sense of vitality and feel emptiness. To be sure, he also underlined the variability in the constitution of this inner self across cultures, in what sustains and defines it, and it was around this point that he finally situated the undecidable debate over the universal applicability of psychoanalytic constructs for understanding human behavior. In essence, he asked, is the inner "soul-self" basically organized, as psychoanalysts have theorized, regardless of context, with equivalent affective states, object-relations structures, and defensive operations, or does the shaping of human behavior by culture extend to the creation of different selves for which familiar Western concepts are not strictly applicable?

Because I cannot very well avoid this issue, I declare my own preference for the fuzzy middle ground, one that rests on a foundation of intrinsic human potentialities and universals of life (birth, injury, pain, comfort, loss), while leaving plenty of space for the differential organization of these givens. Because psychoanalysis has tended naively to favor and assume psychobiologic explanations for the "natural" appearance of emotions, my emphasis in this discussion is on the anthropologist's (and Lacan's) point about the symbolic construction of affect. "Emotion," said Lutz (1988), "is about deep commitments to particular other persons and to seeing events in certain ways" (p. 216). What distinguishes affect from a "cold" cognition, Rosaldo (1984) concluded, is the sense of engagement of the actor's self. "Emotions," she wrote, "are about the ways the social world is one in which we are involved" (p. 143). As Schweder (1991) observed, children have to learn, not the basic vocabulary of emotion, which may be innate, but its syntax. The variegated hills and valleys of a four-year-old's emotion to which he alluded will become smoothed out and structured in development, so that an adult tends to live his affects in a manner recognizable, communicable. and acceptable to the social world of other subjects to which he belongs.

An important subcategory of this discussion in anthropology of particular interest to Lacanians concerns the differential construction of self within different linguistic systems. Rephrased in these terms, the question becomes whether there is one basic human self articulated differently by each linguistic community, or whether the structure of each language dictates an alternative form of self? No doubt this alternative is once again too stark. Human beings cannot be all that different, after all. And yet anyone who has spent time abroad and attempted to penetrate another culture knows that there is always, even in the most similar societies, a residue of otherness from which the visitor feels excluded (see Whorf, 1956). Anthropologists, for example, have noted the extent to which many cultures are strongly sociocentric, deemphasizing individuation in favor of powerful group identities from which the self cannot be separated (see Kurtz, 1992, for a strong presentation of this nonuniversalist argument). Lutz, for instance, described a situation in which she requested a group of Ifaluk women on the small Pacific island where she was living to accompany her to the local well, only to be rewarded with a set of blank, dropped faces for her inappropriate use of the first person singular pronoun to suggest a shared event. Ifaluk society represents a variation on a common theme of submersion and submission to a group identity that is characteristic of many cultures and represents a limiting case for the application of Western notions of individual motivation and responsibility. This perspective was well expressed by Geertz (1974) who wrote:

> The Western conception of the person as a bounded, unique, more or less integrated motivational and cognitive universe, a dynamic center of awareness, emotion, judgement, and action organized into a distinctive whole and set contrastingly both against other such wholes and against its social and natural background is . . . a rather peculiar idea within the context of the world's cultures [p. 126].

Even within our own heterogeneous culture, we know that psychic life is organized variously for different persons and that our psychoanalytic assumption of a shared reality across the range of fellow colleagues and patients is an optimistic and generous gesture, bridging great differences. More pertinent to our discussion, how and when a person experiences affect and the significance it carries for her will depend on features unique to that individual, her life history, and the microenvironment of her family of origin. Along with Schweder, I agree that the common feeling of emptiness and loss is probably similar and infectious across a range of personalities, yet its force, meanings to the person, and consequences are inevitably different and not totally sharable. In the most general terms, we can hypothesize that these variations in quality and structuration of affect represent differential outcomes of the process of symbolization of primary life experiences. That is, intrasubjective psychic experience, beginning preverbally and corporally, undergoes a process in the course of which it becomes "mentalized" or mediated by symbolic processes, and these representations permit intersubjective communication about inner experience to others. The representations and symbols, of course, come from without, from the fund of languaged narratives available in the surrounding culture as they are passed on, primarily by parents, beginning soon after birth. These signifying narratives belong to the Other, to the field of language shared with other members of the relevant social universe to which the subject belongs. They are also private, by their unique links (metonymies) with personal experiences. As Bucci (1985) wrote in this context, "Children learn to 'name,' to attach words to experience, in an interpersonal context in which experience is shared" (p. 594).

The burgeoning and complex field of narrative within psychoanalysis addresses this point (see Shafer, 1992, for a model in many ways relevant to a Lacanian approach). Nothing can be understood or known until it becomes part of a story, and the stories we learn are delivered to us by many hands. Naturally we can only make incomplete sense of much of what is told us, but we pursue coherence, comfort, and satisfaction of various desires in interpreting the narratives available and in creating new ones. The interpersonal context is charged with often enigmatic emotional energies that give their stamp to the language employed. From a Lacanian perspective, there is a materiality to the signifier, a concreteness bound to uniquely personal bodily sources that undermines the rational, intersubjective meaning by which we attempt to contain private experience. Nonetheless, we have no recourse outside the narratives available to us and are obliged as languaged creatures to use them in giving voice to affects as shareable expressions of personal existence.

To the extent that Lacan's concept of the symbolic register is synonymous with culture, it consists of organizing rules and structures that act as a template for the nascent subject. The specific linguistic universe surrounding the child from the moment of birth defines the possible forms of self-organization and thereby at once enables and constrains the possibilities for the expression of core inner experiences, coded, according to Bucci, in concrete, nonlinguistic representations. This brings us to the crucial question of desire raised by Lacan. As a key term in the Lacanian framework for any discussion of vitality and subjective "aliveness," desire describes an essential human characteristic that takes man beyond the purely biological level of the drive or of phylogenetic emotion. Lacan's conception of desire has philosophic roots, notably in Hegel, and he was, at least for the middle period of his theory construction, drawn to the philosopher's parable of the encounter between master and slave as a metaphor for the clash of human desires. In Hegel's mythic story, two subjects each seek an absolute recognition of their own unique individualities from the other. It is in a way a description of the narcissistic dilemma as formulated by Modell (1980) that the self needs the other for affirmation of its existence, yet constantly risks being injured or destroyed by the other's negation. Lacan (1964), influenced by Kojeve's interpretation of the story, wrote, "Man's desire is the desire of the Other" (p. 38). This means that in a two-way dialectic, man desires what the other wants (he wants to assume the other's desire and possess what is coveted by the other), but, at the same time, he desires to be desired by the other (to be the object of the other's desire). Hegel's portrayal of this encounter was a stark one: Either one subject accepts total submission to the other as a slave or he possesses the other in a total, exclusive way that confirms him in his glorious uniqueness as the master. The narcissistic dilemma described by Modell (1980) is the wish to obtain confirmation of an ideal, grandiose self while risking in the process a total collapse of self. As he observed, the other is necessary to confirm the imaginary self but is also a threat to its existence.

Lacan's major theoretical move in the mid-1940s was to attempt a resolution of the Hegelian impasse by recourse to a new principle of the symbolic order, derived from the work of the anthropologist Claude Lévi-Strauss. From this perspective, master and slave are defined mutually by a symbolic field external to them that organizes and structures their relationship. Language with its rules and cultural formulas exemplifies this field, which Lacan also called "the big Other," the third element in any intersubjective encounter. The symbolic field of the Other sets limits and defines the place of each individual subject in the world, obliging the participants in any intersubjective relationship to subsume or modulate their narcissistic desires. Whatever fantasies of greatness or oneness a person may entertain, as a speaking subject he is ultimately constrained by secondary process logic and the reality principle, whose violation brings serious symptoms of psychic disarray. Within the symbolic transference, the Other is represented by the position of the analyst.

For Lacan, the symbolic order does not change the fundamental desire of the subject, which is unconscious, but directs it away from a dyadic, mirroring situation into speech. Desire must now pass through "the narrow defile of the signifier." Lacan defined it as a fundamental demand for love and recognition that arises from the unusual situation of prolonged dependency and helplessness in infancy and the secondary "birth" by separation-individuation from the mother–child matrix as a unique, named subject of language. From a slightly different vantage point, desire is an effect of primordial object loss and the retroactive symbolization of the lost object within language that forms the substrate of the emerging self. The object is longed for but can never be restored as such, only called to within speech. For this reason, desire can never be totally fulfilled within the limits of human communication. At the same time, along with its highly abstract, symbolic features, desire, as Lacan stated, always has libidinal consequences. The notion here is that the human yearning for completeness, beginning when the infant first differentiates the mother as a subject from her function as the object of physiologic, drive needs, never becomes totally divorced from those bodily roots but attaches itself to a pressing physical urge that, unlike desire itself, does hold the possibility of satisfaction. Thus the demandingness of a frustrated toddler for various, seemingly arbitrary objects indicates his painful struggle with desire, when the means of expression are limited. This example, discussed by Lacan (1956–1957), suggests that the toddler's amalgam of need and desire manifests itself in an affective form that takes shape within the infant–mother interaction. Over time, it becomes an increasingly differentiated communication about what the child can say he wants. Given the wide disparity of mothering practices across cultures, it stands to reason that the grammar of this communication will be constructed rather differently. To cite just one example, Kurtz (1992) contrasted the Hindu mother's custom of carrying infants on the hip with the middle-class American style of intermittent, intense, face-to-face gaze. Still other cultures keep a young child on the mother's back. Each of these behaviors has substantial effects on the embodied qualities of early intersubjective experience. More important, the specific dyadic interaction may not go smoothly for many reasons, and the grammar may be inadequate or obscure, so that need and desire fail to be structured in any communicable manner for some children. This can be described in Bucci's (1985) terms as a failure of translation into the linguistic code.

Lacan (1959–1960) attempted to define the ethic of psychoanalysis as never to give up on one's desire (p. 321; *ne jamais céder sur son désir*), desire being idiosyncratic and irreducible. This principle would seem to take him into an exploration of how the thread of affective expression leads toward a better apprehension of desire, but such was not at all the case. A rereading of Lacan in this way might help us better understand the purpose of psychoanalysis, if we discard the reifications of early Freudian theory. The crucial problem for many patients is precisely a loss of contact with desire and an incapacity to be a subject of desire. At the most basic level, this reflects a serious difficulty in managing and expressing affect. When lived experience remains private and uncommunicable—if there are obstacles to symbolic integration—as in the case of Margaret Little, the outcome may be her sense of "total annihilation" in place of a conviction of existence as a person "acknowledged by . . . other people" (Little, 1985, p. 13). Green (1977) in his abbreviated article, "Conceptions of Affect," wrote that the fundamental task of affect is to supply content to what is experienced only in unrepresentable forms. In the presence of an inner void, he observed, intense affect may be the only proof of one's existence. In "Passions and Their Vicissitudes" (1980b), Green went further:

> The fall of the symbol demonstrates the fact that the symbolic order is attached to the subject's very existence, which is not only his reason for living, but his passion to be. In other words, the presence of emblems is the price of life; or, to put it another way, the entire love of life is consubstantial with them [p. 222].

In Lacanian terms, desire that insists along the chain of speech must find its expression in affects, which not only embody the subject, but also convey his historical experience—the symbols he lives by—in language that can be sustained in the universal discourse with others. Affects, Green (1977) suggested, are not simply powerful discharges, but serve as symbolic mediators of inner processes, giving them a voice. Patients lacking this resource are left in the nonexistent position, out of life. Lacan's (1974) insight that the natural habitat of the body is language seems correct. In other words, the human body inhabits a symbolic cultural space that rules its functions to a very great extent. When and what to eat, how and where to sleep, whether to sit or stand, and all the other elementary behaviors of the human species are codified in abstract terms that have no other reality than language. Contra Lacan, however, I would argue that signifiers must offer access to implicit models of experience outside of language, concrete intersubjective experiences, which are no doubt founded in the preverbal, in kinesthesis, and in sensory motor life. In Bucci's (1985) dual coding model, "emotion is linked more closely to perceptual representations" (p. 128). She stated, "painful affect is likely to be associated more intensely with imagery than words. Much of this painful material may never be reproduced in verbal form." Nonetheless, she continued, "language is the means by which private experience, knowable directly only to the patient, can be transmitted to the analyst" (p. 128). Early bodily experiences of self with others (or "self with Other"), shape the organization of desire in specific ways, as Kurtz (1992) suggested. Signifiers are anchored to the body as a permanent dimension of life.

The coding of nonverbal representations seems difficult to subsume under Lacan's model, except as a feature of the imaginary realm of mirrors and images underpinning a false self. Winnicott held a broader view of self-formation, incorporating the holding environment as embodied and the mirror in its intersubjective connotation as the mother's face with the affects it conveys. I believe that this perspective best explains Kohut's concept of the selfobject—that is, an environment mother who sends messages and defines a field within which the subject can take shape. For Winnicott, the delineation of self from other, mediated and buffered by a transitional space, requires the omnipotent illusion of creating the object, which then survives to prove its independent existence. At this point there must be a step into the realm of verbal symbols. The subjective object of Winnicott is the child's creation, developing in concert with a complex set of perceptual and sensory experiences. In contrast, the separate maternal subject (as absent, as not where she was imagined to be) exists within the symbolic order. As a consequence, the origins of love and desire for the other are concurrent with the emergence of self and other in the symbolic realm. Green (1980b) added the element of passion to this formulation, making a connection between the symbolic order, which provides an identity, and "Eros," the love of life or the joy in existing as a subject. This is close to Lacan's (1972–1973) formulation, "we don't know what it is to be alive except for the following fact, that a body is something that enjoys itself" (p. 23). He repeated many times that this corporal enjoyment (*jouissance*) is something we don't know anything about. *Jouissance*, for Lacan, represents the self's longing for a state of being prior to its insertion into the symbolic order that creates the divided human subject, which is a function of the signifier. The problem recognized by Green and Lacan is that Freud's notion of affect as instinctual derivative, thus a biological product, is inadequate. Affect mediates nonverbal bodily experiences by linking them to words. It dwells in the languaged world. In this way, in disagreement with Bucci (1985), I find it more precise to say that these experiences simply "are." In Lacanian terms, they exist in the real of the body, which can only be known indirectly through mediation (even imagery serves this purpose).[1]

---

[1]There are two important issues here that lie outside my present focus. First, there is the question of the organization of imagistic thinking by linguistic structures and whether there is such a thing as nonlanguaged thought. Second, there is the problem of memory as Bucci (1985) posed it. Can there be nonverbal

In this vein, Green (1973) remarked that both ego psychologists and Lacan shared a distrust of affect as an essential component of psychic life and tended to subsume it under cognitive operations (the signal) or the movement of the signifier, respectively. For the Freudians, the signal is a message generated by the ego as a warning about the appearance of a drive derivative. For Lacan, the movement of words (signifiers) carries affect (images and feelings) in its wake, but its causes lie elsewhere (in the Other, in the signifying chain that determines the subject). Lacan took this step because he saw the primacy of the symbolic mode of functioning in the human world and recognized that the existence of the subject depends "kit and caboodle" on some kind of suturing of fragmented inner experience onto symbolic structures, which are by their nature decentering and extrinsic to the individual human being with his idiosyncratic passions and fantasies. At the same time, the corporal juice that lubricates language, the desire that gives it substance and force, is neglected in Lacan's later writings, which seem to depict a disembodied and abstract subject, like an algebraic function. This leads me to suggest another Lacanian reading in which affect holds a signifying function, as the expression of a subject facing the limits of the symbolic order and the gap separating her from a full realization of desire. The prime example of this involves the sexual relationship. "There is no such thing as a sexual relationship," Lacan wrote in many places (for example, see Lacan, 1972–1973, p. 144), meaning that there is no way to symbolize a harmonious, complete relationship, which always falls short of its goal. Man's "exile" from the sexual relation, he proposed, creates the gap-generating affect. "Isn't that tantamount to saying that it is only owing to the affect that results from this gap that something is encountered . . . ?" (p.145). In these passages, Lacan appeared to be speaking about the affect of love, emerging on the level of an intersubjective relationship to fill the defect in realization of fantasy and of drive. The affect of love, like all affects, however, is always accompanied by a story, by models and images that can be expressed and shared.

---

memories based on physical states of the body that are potentially verifiable? This formulation is close to Modell's (1990) position about affective experiences bound to the body, which serve as a reality check on memory. My hunch is that there probably are such imagistic, sensory traces from early life that underlie a few basic concepts like presence or absence and pleasure or unpleasure, and that, possibly, traumatic events are partially coded in this form.

In similar fashion, the affects highlighted by Kohut (idealization of the object, excitement in being seen, and so forth) point to an intersubjective desire. Although animated by passion in that sense, Kohut's conception of the "self" and its emotional states nevertheless seems abstract and disembodied, with an idealized aura. The child desires the mother's empathy, mirroring, and gleam in her eyes, but not, as Lacan might say, "her tits." It is as though a particular cultural version of the subject has been accorded a privileged status. In the larger scheme of things, the firm center of initiative and healthy narcissism of the beaming American self suggested by Kohut's descriptions may turn out to be an aberration. Here we may need an eventual anthropology of psychoanalysis to sort out these contingent elements. In the meantime, a conception of health or normality built upon control and self-realization may be damaging for the field. Affect, as Green never tired of reiterating, always tends toward overflow and disruption. As passion, it goes beyond the expressible and acceptable, even as it paradoxically may strengthen the self. According to Green (1973), in its role as "signifier of the flesh and the flesh of the signifier" (p. 332), affect cannot be severed from the real of its bodily roots.

In the clinical sphere, we often come up against an inability to express affects, perhaps like Margaret Little's silence on the couch. Her difficulty may have been in part the lack of specific mediating words and ideas that Winnicott eventually provided her, but it was also the failure or weakness of the internal intersubjective function that enables private states to be expressed in the presence of another. His belief in the necessity of a profound regressive experience in analysis may have been in part based on his intuition of her need to reestablish this function, which he understood as requiring a reliving of the physical and emotional mix-up of the primary mother–child relationship. A similar story to Little's is told in Winnicott's (1986) account of his analysis of a schizoid young man who was at times silent or asleep but, at other times, simply chattered on in a boring fashion. The patient's striking symptom of empty speech was emphasized in Masud Khan's discussion of the case. The young man, who was not given a name, at one point stated, "I remember a striking difference beween the desire to be silent last time and the desire to get away from chattering. Chatter has limitations. . . . I like the idea of chatter but pure chatter has no edge to it, no purpose. Chatter is talking to no person"

(p. 143). Khan discussed the absence of play in this patient's speech and Winnicott refered to its defensive, false self functions. Presumably, the genuine desire to remain silent implies a true self that cannot be communicated. The problem of this man's nonpresence, however, was never linked explicitly with affect, which Winnicott may have felt was simply too dangerous for someone verging on psychotic decompensation. The patient stated, "I never became human . . . I missed it" (p. 96). What Winnicott did assert was the need for deep regression to recapture the earliest demarcations of self from other, which he interpreted to this patient in what seems a surprisingly intellectualized way.

Today, many of us are uncomfortable with Winnicott's heroic measures, which seem at the least outside the range of most therapists—rightly so, in my opinion. I concur with Modell (1990) that the notion of a literal temporal and psychic regression in itself is questionable. What does seem plausible is that, for many patients, the symbolic function has been damaged; certain links have been broken; certain kinds of risks of communication will not be taken. Among other things, the problem of affect in difficult clinical situations of the type Green, Modell, and Winnicott describe requires reexamination of the function of the ego ideal. As Freud (1914) observed, the ego ideal is the product of internalization of transgenerational codes that regulate personal relationships, mediated through contact with the parental superego. It is the superego (largely unconscious) and not the ego (largely conscious) of the parents that provides the contents of the ego ideal. Lacan (1956–1957) attributed this set of functions to the paternal metaphor, which establishes "the Law." This Law can be identified with the symbolic order itself, which the father in his function as a symbolic object, a "third" of separation from the plenitude of the mother–child dyad, represents. I hypothesize that a failure of paternal mediation, a failure of transmission, is fundamental to disturbances of the ego ideal and its functions. Failure may result either from traumatic intrusion and an excess of parental presence or from absence and psychic death. The father, for example, can violate his symbolic function or abdicate from it. More broadly and accurately, one or both parents, even if physically present, can fail to transmit or uphold the symbolic order (Kirshner, 1992). The place of the father or of any third party is established in the first place by the mother, who recognizes that the child does not belong to her but has an independent legal and social status. Either parent may transgress this limitation by using the child narcissistically as a pure imaginary extension of self. The child's response to such exploitation may then be to construct a false self of his own, out of touch with vital desires and talking an empty and boring speech. This is another reason why the analytic relationship itself takes on so much importance for this type of case. Winnicott (1986) advised pastoral counselors, in fact, that boredom in the presence of a troubled parishioner was the best indication for referral to an analyst!

For patients with a fragile sense of existence and a serious narcissistic vulnerability to fragmentation, the central task of treatment can be reduced to reestablishment of trust in the analyst. One might speak of reaching a regressive position of holding or of a symbolic repetition of a core vulnerable state that reopens the question of basic trust, analogous to Balint's (1968) notion of the basic fault. The early relationship is not literally repeated, but the basic structural flaws previously covered by defenses against relatedness and affect are exposed. The analyst's task, of course, is to respond to this vulnerable self by containing and helping the patient articulate affective expression. In the end, the analyst must be seen as a person operating under a system of values (with an ego ideal), who fulfills a symbolic function, as presumably Winnicott did for Margaret Little (not without dangerous lapses). She must respect her own and the patient's essential limits and recognize the painful history subsumed in their encounter. Perhaps we could speak in this context of a restoration of transmission or of a repair of the intersubjective function of the ego ideal, in part by the analyst symbolizing, through words, her emotional experience within the countertransference. The objective is to contain affective communications until they can be verbalized and shared in the virtual space of the therapeutic relationship. In the next chapter, I make use of these concepts to explore clinical data from analytic practice, where we again confront the complaint of nonexistence.

4

— • —

Trauma, Depression,
and the Sense of Existence

— • —

Is it any wonder that I don't exist?

—Ms. G

IN THIS CHAPTER, I PRESENT CLINICAL MATERIAL FROM TWO ANALYSES TO elaborate on the theoretical issues I have described previously and to develop the relationship between disturbances of the sense of self-cohesion and traumatic experience. To introduce them, I first take up additional elements of the Lacanian theory of trauma and compare them with some contemporary approaches, using principally the work of Phillip Bromberg, which most lucidly articulates a model of therapeutic action similar to my own. Because histories of trauma and states of depression are frequent (though not constant) accompaniments of complaints of "not having a life," in what follows I explore their connections and suggest what Lacan can contribute to our understanding of them.

As clinicians, I believe we should take seriously Schweder's (1991) anthropological insight that what we call depression is a collapse or breakdown of a subjective intrication of self with world. From a position of unself-conscious participation in the unquestioned "reality" of the surrounding social world, the depressed person suddenly feels oddly decentered. In depression, Heidegger's existential state of "thrownness," with all its discomforting strangeness, predominates. We are thrown like an odd-shaped piece into an arbitrary circumstance that no longer feels right, with a sense of disconnection from who we thought we were. Psychoanalysts, of course, have approached this phenomenon mainly through the notions of loss and helplessness. A human or symbolic object (a person, a social role, a set of beliefs or principles) is no longer available in psychic reality as it had been, with immediate consequences for mental functioning. The idea or image may be accessible, but it has become a shell, losing its power to animate and motivate. The subject may complain of a void, a feeling of impotence, or a total loss of initiative. In Lacanian terms, what seems at stake is the relation of the subject to the symbolic order, especially through the link of signifiers to the body and the real, for which I have followed Green in proposing affect as central. From this perspective, we might hypothesize that depressive guilt in its various manifestations represents an attempt to reestablish agency by seeking to reach the lost object (to be worthy of, to suffer for, to punish one's failures toward, and so forth). The fact that every depression is not characterized by these affects indicates the secondary nature of guilt and its essentially compensatory function (as Fairbairn, 1943, argued[1]). People hold onto guilt, said Fairbairn, not so much for masochistic reasons but to preserve the moral authority of the superego.

Although Lacan did not speak much about depression, he can help us better understand what is involved in loss. Here we must take a brief excursion into his view of object relations, or, more precisely, his critique of that theoretical position, based on his well-known model of the three registers of psychic experience: the Imaginary, the Symbolic, and the Real. In chapter 2, we discussed the tension between imaginary and symbolic relations at some length, the central idea being the grounding of the symbolic in speech, in

[1] In this disturbing and original article, Fairbairn addressed the structuring function of guilt, which by implication belongs to the depressive position of whole object relations. The attack by a primordial bad object harkens back to Freud's (1895) speculations in the "Project for a Scientific Psychology" on the origins of the infant's apperception of the other. Where the primary object is poisonous and hateful, in Fairbairn's conception, the sense of hope or goodness is destroyed and the subject feels menaced by death. Lacan's critique of Fairbairn (uncharitable, as usual) emphasized the imaginary nature of his approach, in which everything seems to reduce to fantasy, rather than building on his innovative model to show how the tie to the good object (to the symbolic Other) must be preserved at all cost.

the polysemous chain of discourse that is, on one hand, open-ended (as opposed to the more static images of the mirror relationship) and, on the other hand, limited or directed by the important signifiers received by the subject from the Other (from the parents, for all practical purposes). Lacan's third register of the real is perhaps most difficult to conceive but can be briefly defined as that which is excluded from symbolization and fantasy and cannot be assimilated into these functions. It refers to what inevitably cannot be captured in symbols of "reality" and to what seems to resist symbolization. For Lacan, the "object" as such does not have a true "essential" existence but is an unstable mental composite of these three registers, each of which attempts to circumscribe it in a different way, corresponding to their respective functions. Thus, the ego, as discussed in chapter 2, as an agency of the imaginary, seeks substantive mirroring objects to affirm its self-definition as a discrete entity, while the "I" expressed in the open flow of verbal communication pursues less definable symbolic objects of desire.

In essence, the subject or "self" (the term can be used here without undue distortion of Lacan's point) is empty. At the place where a signifier of self that could define the identity of the subject might reside in the unconscious (the answer to the question, "Who am I?"), there is only a lack, which fantasy attempts to fill. Narcissistic fantasies define the operation of the ego as constantly attempting to promote a substantial full self, which is by definition illusory. In contrast to this imaginary solution, the Lacanian subject leans on a symbolic identification, which installs her difference from other subjects as another "one."[2] Following Freud's comments on the

---

[2]Lacan's psychoanalytic approach to understanding the nature of the subject partook of a philosophic tradition that had been renewed in France through the seminar of Kojeve on Hegel's phenomenology, translations from Heidegger, and the competing reading of these authors by Sartre, who emphasized in a more closely argued way the thesis of the emptiness of the self. The innovation of Lacan was to center his approach around the nature of language. With his concepts of the unitary trait, which marks the subject, and of the binary signifier, instituting the signifying chain, discussed in Seminar IV (1956–1957) and Seminar VIII (1960–1961) among other places, Lacan develops and greatly modifies Freud's (1921) relatively minor point on identification based on a single feature (*einziger Zug*), mentioned in "Group Psychology and the Analysis of the Ego." For Lacan, the single trait taken from the father is represented by a signifier that installs a symbolic identification.

origins of the superego and ego ideal, I believe we can extrapolate Lacan's version of symbolic identification to refer to the link between the subject and the surrounding cultural world of meanings by means of which the subject is stitched onto social reality. One definition of depression is that it describes the state of the person following damage to this link.

In today's "postmodern" psychoanalytic climate, the deconstruction of the notion of a substantial self has become a familiar feature of many theories, notably those of Mitchell (1991) and Bromberg (1994) within the interpersonal tradition and Ogden (1994) within the modern Kleinian movement. Bromberg and Kennedy (1997) stressed dissociation of intolerable or unacceptable experiences (commonly those associated with physical or sexual abuse) into sequestered loci of subjective organization, which is thereby rendered multiple. Although there are many points of convergence with Lacan acknowledged by these authors, there are, of course, important differences. The concept of dissociation represents a metaphor, which, if reified, suggests separate discrete selves that, at the limit, do not communicate, as in some theories of multiple personality disorder. Bromberg's appealing formulation of a subject "standing in the spaces" between these loci raises the question of who is standing. In general, spacial metaphors, useful as they can be in portraying a complex set of variables, foster a pseudovisualization of the psyche, which can support imaginary notions of a "thinglike self." On the other hand, Bromberg's principle of "unfreezing narratives" brings things back to where they belong in discursive reality.

Lacan's difficult concept of the Real supplements these formulations. Essentially, the Real needs to be conceived as referring to the body at a level of corporal experience that is pre- or nonverbal. For Lacan, all human experience revolves around an unassimilable kernel of the real, which simultaneously threatens and supports the symbolic order. To recall, language, as a system of differential sounds sliding over concepts to which they refer more or less loosely, carves up the undifferentiated facticity of physical reality. For human beings, "every reality is founded by a discourse" (Lacan, 1972–1973, p. 32). Without a discourse, we have no access to the real "thing" behind experience. Lacan's aphorism that what cannot be symbolized returns in the real,[3] resembles Bromberg's thesis of split-off psychic elements.[4] The hopeful therapeutic side of this conception is that the lost experience, returning in the real as repetition, hallucinations, or as symptoms in the body, can be recaptured through actualization in the transference. The Lacanian analyst, Harari (2001) insists that there is no true analysis, properly speaking, "if acting-out by the analysand does not take place during the course of the analysis" (p. 86). Similarly, Bromberg (1994) concludes, "for traumatic experience to be cognitively symbolized it has to be reenacted in a relationship that replays the interpersonal context without blindly reproducing the original outcome" (p. 538). Although there is an important difference between Bromberg's emphasis on the relational context, with implicit participation by the analyst, and the standard Lacanian approach in which the analyst remains remote and relatively unresponsive,[5] I cannot make sense out of Lacan's argument without assuming a connection between something coming from the side of the analyst and its counterpart from the patient's unconscious that creates the need to act out. It is clear from Harari's (2001) discussion that the acting out to which he refers results from a failure of the analyst that provokes a more urgent communication on the part of the analysand. For Bromberg (1994), the relational context reproduces the painful situation that had originally led to dissociation, thereby permitting a reopened dialogue between previously noncommunicating parts of the self, with the subject now "standing in the spaces." This picture seems compatible with the Lacanian notion, elaborated in his Schema L, of the subject moving freely

---

[3]Lacan (1964) discussed trauma in relation to the real in his discussion of the Wolfman case. "At the origin of the analytic experience," he said, "the real presented itself in the form of that which is unassimilable in it in the form of the trauma, determining all that follows and imposing an apparently accidental origin" (p. 55).

[4]Bromberg also referred to Ferenczi's work, which is at the heart of the paradigm shift in contemporary analysis toward attention to the analyst's experience and participation. Lacan treats their metaphor of "split off" in terms of a failure of symbolization (Kirshner, 1994).

[5]See Apollon, Bergeron, and Cantin (2002) for a strong presentation of the rationale for and clinical application of this position.

around a set of possible positions[6] in a structure from which he can speak.

Lacan has something novel to tell us in his vision of a "real" that inevitably must escape symbolization. In this conception, the symbolic order cannot map totally onto reality (can never recapture all of the lost experience, for example). Žižek (1992) explains this issue as follows: The symbolic in its many linguistic/cultural versions covers the realm of the real completely, so that no culture has access to a part of reality which is not conceivable for any other (although it may be valued and thought about quite differently). At the same time, every symbolic system possesses a signifier that, like Freud's "navel of the dream," touches upon the unknown and demands a supernatural authorization. The point here for Žižek is that the figure of God, for example, that underpins the entire logic of the Judeo–Christian–Moslem symbolic belongs to the unsymbolized real. God represents a place in the symbolic where the chain of arbitrary signifiers is quilted down to an ineffable substrate of reality (that is, God really exists).

At the level of the individual subject, this kernel of the real also operates as a basic support, not necessarily in the supernatural sense of God authorizing our personal existence (although this is obviously one common construction), but more as a limit-setting foundation. To explain this, we recall Lacan's insistence on our constant attempt as subjects to repair a fundamental human lack and indeterminacy by pinning the flow of discourse to fantasies (including those that structure the body image), which we attempt to actualize. Ultimately, of course, the speaking subject is embodied. The physical body is a constant substrate on which we found our existence, even though we have no direct access to it in the real but depend on signifiers to represent it for us. Beneath the categories supplied by language and metaphor, however, when we bracket our socially constructed and imaginary body images, there remains a trace of the real of the un- (or pre-) symbolized body. Something of the real remains unmastered, imposing its disturbing presence

---

[6]In my article "A Postmodern Realism for Psychoanalysis" (Kirshner, 1999), I attempted to elaborate this point. A self cannot be "restored," but the subject can enjoy the freedom to move around the determining structure that sustains him. I discussed Lacan's depiction of the subject in schema L in "The Concept of the Self in Philosophy and Psychoanalysis" (1991).

within the symbolic universe. Žižek comments on the dual nature of this trace or "stain" of the real on the social fabric, as at once the guarantee of a sense of certainty of existence (and, no doubt, accounting for it in a way that mere thought cannot) as well as a potential source of disruption of our subjective coherence. We can see the latter effect in the psychotic, for whom "reality," in the form of omnipresent hallucinatory messages and delusional links, constantly threatens to invade private experience up to the extreme of beliefs of body and thought control by the Other. The psychotic subject thus teeters on the verge of collapse into a pure "thing," determined entirely by external, "real" forces. He believes that his unpleasant thoughts and feelings belong to the real, not to his private subjective existence.[7]

A more ordinary example is Lacan's (1954–1955) interpretation of Freud's (1900) famous Irma dream. In the dream, during a reception at which his most important friends and adversaries seem convoked to attack and mock his discoveries, Freud peers into the raw throat of his patient Irma, where he glimpses the formless flesh of her inner body, an unmediated confrontation with the real that lies beneath his theory and science. This, Lacan suggested, is where his pursuit of the secret of hysteria (metaphorical speech, symbolic sensations, sexuality) has taken Freud, and he does not shrink (or awaken) from this encounter, as most of us might. It is a direct encounter with the corporeal real beneath Irma's symptom. Every medical student knows the overwhelming inaugural experience of confrontation with a corpse and its uncanny, inert presence, albeit veiled in wrappings and scientific discourse. Funerals, scenes of injury or diaster, wartime trauma, and other limit situations can also produce transient derealization and subjective fraying with a momentary (or extended) loss of landmarks and reference points that ordinarily cover over the real with familiar symbols. Approached from this perspective, loss inevitably evokes the real, either in the sense of a lost object that has supported our existence (the link with a parent or close relation that directly touches our biological life) or of an intrusive reminder of our presubjective, bodily

---

[7]In his seminar on the psychoses (1955–1956), Lacan presented his metaphor of the *point de capiton* discussed in chapter 2. These "quiltings" of signifiers to signifieds anchor the normal subject to symbolic reality and presumably to the real as well (to a real referent).

foundation (for example, loss of a function or damage to the body). Symbolic loss, of course, can be considered to involve an underlying (sublimated) body function or a vital tie to the other.

To summarize the Lacanian position, self-maintainance (a sense of embodied existence) entails preservation of a certain equilibrium with the real. The subject must preserve contact with the traces of the "thing" (the unsymbolized part of the real), without being overwhelmed by it. Clearly, the multiple sutures of the subject onto a symbolic framework, which I have defined as operating through identifications in the ego ideal, help contain this trace of the real. Conversely, a failure or weakness of these linkages exposes the subject to destabilization by a real that cannot be contained or represented. Here, the Bromberg–Kennedy thesis assumes full value. Incestuous relationships and physical abuse effectively puncture the symbolic envelope around the child with direct biological force (for instance, by treating him as a pure thing) and thereby blur the distinction between fantasy, symbolism, and reality.[8] Abuse of this kind amounts to the enactment of a fantasy "in the real" through exploitation of his or her symbolic power by a parent, teacher, or priest. Attacks on persons or signifiers representing the symbolic order can have a similar result of damaging the subject's linkages to affective discourse. Under such circumstances, depression can be an attempt to remove the self from a reality that is assaultive and castastrophic (for example, the "empty" depressions without affect or ideation, see Green, 1975). Another way to describe this is to say that a depressive sense of nonexistence may be protective against total disintegration in the form of madness or a suicidal desire for death and stakes a claim on an existence that has been lost.

THE CASES OF MR. L AND MS. G

In the following section, I discuss two case histories to further explore the relevance of these concepts of trauma. Granting the highly inexact fit between theory and practice in psychoanalysis and the limitations of selective reporting of cases, I hope at least to convey

---

[8]This puncturing of the symbolic could be a psychoanalytic definition of trauma, as I proposed in an earlier paper (Kirshner, 1994).

how I utilize Lacanian constructs to make my way through analytic work with a group of patients who complain of problems of not feeling intact and present in the world. Although issues that suggest an enfeebled or fragile self arise often and can present in many ways, they emerge with much more clarity in patients troubled by a sense of nonexistence or of "not really being alive." This was the presenting complaint of two individuals, Ms. G and Mr. L, portions of whose analyses I now discuss. These were lengthy treatments, but a few major themes seemed to me to lend themselves to the fundamental questions of "having a life."

Like many of those who speak explicitly about lacking a sense of life, both patients in their initial contacts with me appeared cut off from their affects and expressed detachment and alienation from the world around them. Although depressed, they did not demonstrate the extreme melancholy with which other such "nonexisting" persons, like Margaret Little or the philosopher, Louis Althusser, were afflicted. In some ways, they demonstrate the empty type of depression, a kind of deadness of spirit more profound than a simple state of neurotic inhibition. Ms. G, a 35-year-old professional, had withdrawn from all involvements except caretaking her young child, stating that she felt like "a nullity" and insisting on her ephemeral sense of presence through many similar metaphorical expressions. She wrote in a journal that she shared with me, "Is it any wonder, then, that I don't exist?" Likewise, Mr. L, a married 38-year-old accountant, reported that he was "just going through the motions of life." He felt like a spectator on his own existence, declaring, "I'm not really in life at all."

In thinking about empty depression, I found helpful Green's (1975) description of a protective emptying of the self, in which object relations are attenuated or abandoned in a desperate effort to reinstate a kind of primary narcissism, safe from the threats of intrusion or abandonment by the object. He described a "negative hallucination" of the self, which I take as referring to phenomena like my patients' complaints of nonexistence. They reported as well a general loss of desire in sexuality, personal goals, and life interests, with little available fantasy life. Citing a patient's complaint, *Ça ne chante pas* (it doesn't sing), Green (1999) commented, "This is one of the most mysterious things: why the playing stops, or the song stops, or the vitality disappears" (p. 57). In Lacanian terms, this state of affairs suggests effects of a traumatic real without symbolic means of expression. In a succeeding phase of the analyses I describe, however, there was a dramatic change, in which the patients relinquished their defensive stance of noncommunication of affects and gradually became overwhelmed by intolerable feelings. This shift produced a rather chaotic interaction that was as difficult to support as the previous emptiness.[9] At last, after lengthy work, in a third phase, they were able to find means to bear their emotions and to speak about them in a more integrative manner. I regard their impaired capacities to symbolize and communicate affective states (to knit the traumatic real to the symbolic) as the central psychological problem underlying the phenomenology of "not having a life."

MR. L

Mr. L, whose case I now discuss in more depth, informed me that he could provide the details of a history he knew would be interesting to me, but for him was dead ground, a world of empty facts. His parents, severely traumatized Holocaust survivors who had lost virtually everything, had brought him to the United States at age 11 where they entrusted him to an ultraorthodox Jewish educational system favored by the father. The family lived isolated in a poor neighborhood, and Mr. L spent a lot of time alone, daydreaming. His mother, a depressed and embittered woman, was scornful of Judaism and disparaged American society. These attitudes appeared to extend to her husband, whose religious piety and enjoyment of shared observances with fellow Jews she mocked. The deep

---

[9]Green relates states of empty depression to "decathexis," meaning a withdrawal of psychic energy (libido). "When you undergo depression," Green (1999) writes, "you understand that what you thought were normal processes in life are loaded with cathexis. . . . All this means that you have a permanent flow of energy that you put into these activities. . . . You really discover cathexes when you have lost them" (p. 55). For Lacan, the term "desire" derives not from the Id, but is contingent on language and inherent in the metonymy of symbolic activity as it creates the speaking subject. Biological energies or drives are then utilized secondarily. Green's view retains the corporeal "juice" of the drives, but has the problem of the shaky scientific status of Freudian biology. Lacan grounds his theory in what is specifically human in language and culture, but does seem to lose touch with the phenomenology of lived bodily experience that he mistrusted as a guide.

schism between the parents rendered Mr. L's identification with this simple, religious man, who died three years after immigrating, problematic. On one hand, he struggled with a devalued image of his father as a weak Jewish victim, based on stories of his abject existence in hiding from the Nazis and of his evident passivity and ineffectiveness both in the new country, where he had difficulty with the language, and in the home, where mother was the dominant and scornful person. Father's progressive illness with rectal cancer when the patient was 14 years old reinforced these images of weakness. On the other hand, Mr. L recognized his father's warmth and humor outside the home and for a long time devoted himself to studies in the yeshiva as his father had encouraged. Ultimately, it seemed that the important signifier, "Jew," was compromised as a support for his symbolic identification, just as the paternal role itself seemed to have been within the household.

Starting very young, at least by age nine, Mr. L was having disturbing sexual fantasies with anal content, sometimes stimulated by pictures of nude victims of Holocaust atrocities. These fantasies aroused enormous guilt and a sense of unworthiness, fueling his compliance with religious ritual as he entered his teens. Despite the reassurance provided by his observances, however, he felt himself to be emotionally abused at the orthodox school where he was educated, developing a consuming hatred for the rabbis there, who seemed hypocritical and sadistic to him, even as he depended emotionally and intellectually upon the structure they provided. One could say that the tragedy of his parents and of the world from which they came was played out in sexualized terms within his restricted Jewish environment. To be humiliated or to be degraded—ultimately by anal penetration—seemed to be the fate of the weak and passive. As he was to express it many times, Mr. L grew up in a medieval world with its earthy sensuality of odors, physical closeness, and mysticism that offered him shelter and acceptance away from his own sad family and the foreign society around them. Yet, looking at the yeshiva through the gaze of the "other," he felt contempt and rage. When he much later made his departure from that world, he saw himself as an alien in modern America with a secret, shameful past. Away from home for the first time at graduate school in his twenties, he pursued intense sexual relationships to combat a deepening sense of isolation and deadness. A sense of despair was never far away, however, and, with a gradual drifting away from his religious commitments, a sense of unreality and of leading an unreal life began to pervade his experience. After graduation, in part to flee from these feelings, Mr. L married a Jewish woman for whom he felt no passion and settled down to lead a superficially normal life. It was out of a growing sense of an inner void and of existing "outside of life" that he decided to seek treatment, ultimately psychoanalysis.

Mr. L did have a fascinating and dramatic history, but he did not begin to come alive for himself or to move in the analysis until our work on transference resistances and resistance to transference (he wanted to protect me and himself from what he knew lay underneath) began to permit what became an ever more violent and archaic expression of his sadistic impulses. The story he told with detachment at the beginning of analysis then became a passionate outpouring of hatred and contempt for his parents and teachers accompanied by a recitation of sexual fantasies, in extreme contrast to his previous flat and depressive demeanor. At this point, his experience of depersonalization gave way to a panicky and desperate state in which, one might say, his imaginary fantasy life became plastered up against his sense of external reality in a way that left little space for symbolic elaboration or differentiation of the two domains. In psychotic-like rages filled with scatological terms, Mr. L vomited or defecated speech that seemed filled with presence and action. Frequently, he rushed from his car directly to my office bathroom toilet. En route to one session, he had an episode of encopresis. "I'm bringing you my shit," he joked. Here, we could refer to a disruptive return of trauma in the real in a concrete fecal form as a part of his own body, linked to pleasure as the unsymbolized lost part object, partly representing a gift to the Other in the transference via an acting out (Lacan's *objet petit a*, which I will explore in chapter 5, seemed in play). Mr. L's eruption in action was destabilizing and anxiety producing, but also strangely exciting for him. To reverse the Freudian dictum, "Where Id was there shall Ego be," we might say, "Where I thought I was, I no longer am," or, as Žižek (1992) rephrased it, "The story I have been telling about myself to myself no longer makes sense" (p. 162).

In fact, Mr. L described depersonalization feelings after his anal outbursts, and, at times, his diatribes against the rabbis took on paranoid dimensions, a slippage from his usual exacting reality testing. He was "not himself." Driving his car along back roads, where he could stop to relieve himself, he saw the world in a Swiftian vision of excrement, roamed by human cattle depositing their loads. These ravings were not psychotic because they held to a metaphoric frame, one in which the historical symbolic referents were all too clear (cattle, filth, and so forth). Moreover, he could create a kind of grim humor and thereby experience pleasure (which entails a nonpsychotic structure). In this sense, his anal self could be viewed in Bromberg's terms as dissociated and seeking to compose its narrative (directed to the Other in the transference).

Loewald (1980) cited Valery's observation that poetry restores to language "those things that tears, cries, and caresses try obscurely to express" (p. 204). Although Mr. L's diatribes were not in the least poetic, his switch from empty to intensely charged emotive speech illustrates the inherent dilemma of the subject striving to sustain a discourse. Affect may be the flesh of the signifier, yet as pure discharge, it can obliterate the symbolic framework that differentiates self from objects. This is a familiar problem in the treatment of many borderline patients, whose explosions of emotion can be overwhelming and lead to self-destructive action. In Mr. L's case, verbal expression of hateful anal rape fantasies, fusing early memories, parental accounts of the Holocaust, and his own pornographic sexual interests, were not tenable. He felt like "a murderous shit who deserved destruction." Had this process not occured within the safe, if precarious, setting of analysis, Mr. L might well have acted on the suicidal feelings he so often expressed. Conversely, his rigid character defenses against this otherness within himself had left him in an equally untenable position of a deadened, "lifeless nimbleness." In my own countertransference position, initial reactions of fascination and concern with the flood of negative affects gave way to feelings of hopelessness and emptiness, for which at moments I began to hate the patient. My highly invested embrace of the analytic role as one supporting value and meaning carried me through difficult periods, although it may also have restricted my capacity to receive more fully the primitive communications he expressed. These issues are further elaborated in what follows.

MS. G

Ms. G had similar problems with reality. She dreamed repeatedly of raising her head from a washbasin to confront a featureless and empty visage, as though approaching the status of a desubjectivised "thing," a pure stain of the real. This dizzying sense of losing her self was repeated at certain moments in the transference, when she felt that she existed only in my presence. She had fantasies of transforming herself into a small statuette, which I could carry in my pocket, or at least allow to be left inside my office, almost as if she sought to attach herself to my imaginary body. The analyst, she was certain, did exist, but her fantasies suggested that I represented the omniscient *sujet supposé savoir* (the supposed subject of knowledge) of Lacan, who, possessing signifiers of his identity, is part of the impossible real.[10] Another way to say this is that the patient imputes to the analyst answers to basic existential questions which would restore a complete self—a perfected self that is not attainable within the limits of the symbolic order.

In Ms. G's case, her tenuous grip on her personal reality was revealed in many ways. A long-term struggle with bulimia had resulted in a roller coaster history of enormous weight gains and losses, so she could joke that she had gained and lost herself dozens of times. "Is it any wonder that I don't exist?" she wrote in a poem. Indeed, she often used drawings and poems to convey a precarious and evanescent sense of her own presence, which seemed belied by a history of acting out in which she could be in turn cruel, seductive, or self-destructive. The attraction she could exercise on men when she was thin fascinated and enraged her, and in the past had often produced sadomasochistic encounters from which she would emerge exhilarated and terrified. In those situations, such as an encounter with a North African porter on a European train or shady characters in clubs, she could be extremely sexually provocative, only to turn scornfully on the men when they moved to respond to her invitation. This had resulted in truly dangerous situations for her. When similar wishes surfaced in the transference, her analysis was threatened and she felt compelled to isolate herself as before.

---

[10]The analyst in the symbolic transference represented the Other for Lacan, holding the place of the supernatural signifier of the real—the place of the master who "knows" (see Zizek 1992, pp. 102–104).

For example, once entering the office for a Monday session, she began teasing me about the belt buckle I was wearing, using a coy tone I had not previously heard. She asked if she could touch it, extending her hand, and then withdrew abruptly into prolonged silence on the couch. Although I immediately was aware of the teasing scenario she had previously recounted, I was momentarily without words, with the sense that anything I might say would be humiliating or sadistic. Later I jotted down the phrase, "in the grip of a projective identification." Whatever this phrase might actually mean, I have come to think of this type of event as a complex communication using certain cultural stereotypes—a spanking or whipping, a flirtation, a defiance—known to each of us and conveying a set of attitudes involving fear, desire, use of power, violation, and other sensations, perhaps approaching what a young child might implicitly understand but be unable to say. Later, we realized that her seductive behavior was connected to the fantasies of becoming a statuette in my pocket. This worked as follows: As object of a seduction (in the objectifying gaze of the train porter or bar pick-up), she thought of herself as a sexual "thing," an entity to be physically used (perhaps one vital to the user). This restaged a piece of the real, as we will see, and temporarily mobilized a sense of existing as an embodied sexual being (it was not simply a mirroring state). At the same time, it threatened to explode that existence, to plunge it into pure "thingness."

Ms. G spent many sessions ridiculing and excoriating her conventional appearing but rather strange parents, who, by her description, seemed totally incapable of raising children. Her mother was a self-absorbed nonpresence, whom she imagined masturbating under the covers while Ms. G attempted to gain her attention as a child, and father was a scientist who conducted her upbringing like a laboratory project in operant conditioning. Frequent affectless physical punishment, including beatings on the buttocks while he pursued her with a strap, in an atmosphere of pseudoreasonableness, left her with intense feelings of rage and humiliation, which she discharged in sexual fantasies and, at an early age, in sexual acts. For example, she manipulated a younger boy into allowing her to undress him and touch his genitals from the rear and also commanded him to masturbate her while she crawled under a table away from him. To what extent were these behaviors sexualized repetitions of father's punishments and to what extent expressions of her awareness of his unconscious sexual interest in the spankings? There were additional indications from later in her development of father's disguised libidinal pleasure in her body, which were acted out in complicit episodes of physical exposure to him. As an adolescent, she staged a scene suggesting unconscious identification with the mother of her earlier fantasies by masturbating while father talked to her outside her door. She also found herself in situations in which men exposed themselves to her, for example in movie theaters, which she cut school to attend. Some of her teenage behavior had the flavor of a prostitution fantasy. "What does this other desire of me?" seemed to be her constant question. All too often, taking the part of an object of desire was apparently the best she could do to affirm herself.[11]

Through his repeated, intrusive punishments, Mr. G (the father) may have offered her a pseudorecognition or sense of her own importance to him that she yearned for as a child, but the price was engagement in quasiperverse scenarios of spankings and whippings. In adolescence, she fled his presence, but seemed drawn to reenact their relationship outside the home. At a relatively young age, she married a devoted older man who was protective and made few demands, even when her fear of repetition forced her to keep him at a physical and emotional distance. During the analysis, when the old fantasies associated with her abuse again threatened to spill over into action, as in the incident of the belt buckle or in similar situations with male colleagues at work, Ms. G became frightened and withdrew home to her bedroom. At those times, she needed to communicate with me by writing to maintain contact. It seemed that, at such moments, speech could become once again a pure instrument of discharge (speaking about the belt buckle, for instance, on the model of "verbalizing a fantasy," became equivalent to enacting it).

COURSE OF THE ANALYSES

For both Mr. L and Ms. G, the analytic experience evolved from an initial flat or depressive period into a phase of intense negative

---

[11]The notion here is that she had never been recognized in her own desire, which, I hypothesize, lay in the wreckage of a collapsed symbolic structure, damaged by early abuse.

emotions, often bound to perverse sexual fantasies. The eruptive surge of emotion and action I saw in this second phase of analysis, as it replaced the initial "psychic death of an ego starved for affect" (Green, 1973, p. 226), could scarcely be contained; it rendered subjective organization or signifying discourse extremely problematic and seeming to threaten a more serious regression. Although the material appeared to point to the way in which their fantasies carried an historical (symbolic) truth, intertwined with an imaginary sadomasochistic scenario, communication of a message or intention in these hours took second place behind discharge into nonverbal behaviors. At times, the "I" of the speaker seemed reduced to its most elemental components, like the scream of a distressed infant approaching the presymbolic real. Perhaps it would be more accurate to say that the "message" communicated in these sessions had to do with collapse of structure and the ensuing exposure of a point of trauma at which language to speak about overwhelming experiences was lacking.

Ms. G's acting in the session was a signal of danger. The belt buckle condensed a sexual with a punitive reference, reminiscent of Freud's (1919) "A Child Is Being Beaten," which suggests her early history of masturbation, itself an echo of the earlier beatings. In Lacanian terms, the significance of the phallus seemed in play, albeit in the form of a dangerous conflation of the imaginary with the real object, evoking the unmastered trauma. That is, Ms. G's father had transgressed his symbolic role by violating her bodily space, interfering with the paternal function of separation and entry into the symbolic order by imposing what was apparently a perverse desire upon her. The object cause of desire (this concept is further elaborated in chapter 5) appeared to be represented by the penis, but as the organ of a young child's fantasies. The repetitive acting out (in theaters, with strange men, and so forth) seemed to blur the metaphoric status of the phallus (signifying lack) with its imaginary one, representing completion, fusion with the Other, and loss of subjective integrity. For this reason, her acting never led to sexual contact, about which she was phobic, but generated enormous anxiety and seemed to threaten a more drastic loss or fragmentation of self.

In chapter 3, I argued that for Lacan and Kohut, a quest for self-affirmation through a selfobject or mirroring partner (a narcissistic object relationship) was a response to the threat of fragmentation. Most contemporary analysts would probably agree that an empathic stance, which meets this need by mirroring the patient, is a necessary and proper technique in similar situations. Nonetheless, although the selfobject relationship and the imaginary transference that underlies it may appear to stabilize the patient (or her ego), Lacan argued that they do not solve the underlying problem and may even represent a clinging to old symptoms and failed solutions. The therapeutic challenge is how to move beyond the empathic holding of a set of reparative or defensive fantasies without reinjuring a very vulnerable patient. In my attempted integration of Kohut with Lacan, I suggested that an empathic position that fosters reconstruction of a deficient selfobject function might permit the eventual reestablishment of a symbolic link to values and intersubjective relationships (beyond the mirror). I think of this process as navigating the mirror relationship without being stranded within it, and I hope to demonstrate this model in what follows.

Mr. L had for years clung to a ritualized form of Judaism that was apparently not deeply felt but rather supported a kind of false self, which could be understood, in part, as an attempt to mirror his orthodox father and teachers. From a Lacanian perspective, Mr. L identified with the set of images and attitudes that were available to him to define a "self" that was inevitably a defensive or false self. Notably, his Jewish identity was saturated with fantasies of imaginary relationships as either victim or persecutor, which seemed to admit of no alternative life possibilities. He referred over and over again to scenarios derived from his parents' accounts of their experiences during the war or from lessons told by his Yeshiva teachers that involved many versions of a dyadic encounter between a helpless Jewish victim and a persecutor, occasionally alternating with a revenge fantasy. At times during his rages, Mr. L would even assume the persecutory position directly, reviling his former orthodox masters (by whom he had felt mistreated) in neo-Nazi language, calling them filth, swine, parasites, and other racist terms. It was difficult to detect the functioning of an effective ego ideal in this simplified (binary) self-structure or any connection with a symbolic order outside the realm of narcissistic fantasy (there was no symbolic structure within which victim–persecutor roles could be relativized or surpassed). Rather I heard the pleasureless repetition of sadomasochistic stories with their monotonous pairings. Albert Camus (1948) once spoke of the need for modern man to reject both these alternatives by confronting the traumatic realities of the war and eschewing grandiose or utopian solutions in favor of a broader human identity. He was aware of the dangers of taking this step of greater uncertainty and risk, which I would summarize as a potential loss of self upon failure of the pole of ideals (that humanity might not uphold) and a kind of veering away of the arc of ambition toward idiosyncratic fantasy.

Ms. G's case was different from Mr. L in that she had previously established a meaningful role in an occupation for which, despite a lack of formal training, she was gifted. Her duties there seemed to involve genuine commitment and pride in activities beyond her own narcissistic interests. However, this engagement, which could be viewed as a strong connection to Kohut's pole of ideals, became undermined by the progressive intrusion of sexual fantasies about colleagues or clients analogous to Mr. L's, and, at a certain point, she found herself unable to continue working. Like him, she was drawn to the abuser–victim dyad as an imaginary model for all relationships. Just as Mr. L was able to gain a sense of male vitality through perverse fantasies, for example, about victims of Nazi soldiers, Ms. G sought the stimulation of sadomasochistic encounters in which she too felt alive and possessed of a sexual identity. When she could succeed in seducing someone (which she experienced at times as an almost irresistible impulse), she felt a renewed sense of vitality and power, provided she could maintain control and avoid the possibility of an actual sexual encounter. Earlier in this chapter, I explored these actings from the perspective of the Lacanian real (the need for repetition of unsymbolized trauma that brings the body back onto the stage). Fantasy enactments also illustrate the concept of a defensive function of mirror solutions to the threat of fragmentation and loss of self. From this perspective, reciprocal sadomasochistic images of self and object (the mirror relation) provided a kind of stabilization and cohesion for Mr. L and Ms. G, but left them with a sense of inauthenticity and constantly risked spilling over into overstimulation and action (in lived reality, of course, the strands of the three Lacanian registers of Imaginary, Symbolic, and Real are inextricably woven together).

Seen through a Kohutian lens, both analysands demonstrate the difficulty of sustaining self-cohesion when affect, "signifier of the flesh," fails to be mediated and given narrative shape by the symbolic structure of "the pole of ideals" or of the ego ideal. One could see this failure reflected in the profound disillusionment and alienation from human relationships and cultural activities reported by Mr. L and Ms. G. On one level, chronic failures of their primary objects and traumatogenic events had disrupted the establishment and maintainance of these mediating functions, which depend upon symbolic identifications. They expressed cynical and bitter attitudes toward their lives, struggling constantly with feelings of emptiness and meaninglessness. Repeated attacks on their objects through accusations of hypocrisy and falseness characterized a transitional period of their analyses, during which they attempted to convey the terrible void in their existence. Erik Erikson's profound concept of basic trust is again relevant to this situation, particularly in the sense in which his schema requires a continual reworking and reestablishment of trust at every developmental stage. Basic trust is the result of ongoing exchanges with others who respond with adequate recognition and empathy, fulfilling age-appropriate needs for such activity. Over time, parental responsiveness must inevitably strike a balance between developmental misattunements and reasonably good matches and between intrusion and sensitive responsiveness, which, if "good enough," anchor the child in the symbolic world of defined roles, social structures, and individual boundaries established in the family. In an analogous way, my hypothesis of a failed connection to the symbolic order, via its internal representations in the ego ideal, does not refer to a reified or static deficit or to a damaged concrete structure, but is the outcome of a process unfolding in time within a real context. As discussed in chapter 2, the Lacanian perspective privileges the paternal function in developing this process, by opening a symbolic space of triangulation. At the same time (and this may represent an omission in Lacan's writings[12]), it is the good-enough mother who supports this function by remaining herself within the limits of the symbolic

---

[12]This would have to be an understatement. Granted Lacan's aim to formalize psychoanalytic theory and avoid sentimentalizing or assuming some kind of natural harmony in human relationships, his replacement of the figure of the mother by the Other and by the concept of *das Ding* and his subsuming mother issues under the retroactive effect of castration produce a striking effect of scotoma. Barzilai (1999) nicely documented this evacuation of mother from Lacanian theory.

maternal role, by her transmission of language and custom, and by establishing a place for the "third," thus validating the father's place.

In the case of Mr. L, the harshness of his denunciation of Jewish orthodoxy and his cynicism about American values and institutions echoed a maternal discourse for which he had become the mouthpiece, an extension of his mother and perhaps a vital prop for her. Even in their infrequent contemporary interactions, he reported feeling either "nonexistent" or as part of some fantasy of hers that excluded all others, including his wife. In her intrusive presence, a transitional space for his subjectivity collapsed, as he moved defensively into what Green (1975) called "a negative hallucination of self" (p. 55) in which he disavowed personal desires or interests and even pretended to share her thoughts and opinions. By negating his presence as a desiring subject, he kept a distance, balanced tenuously between merger and total isolation. This position extended to other important relationships, in a version of Modell's (1984) "sphere within a sphere" (p. 34) set-up, in which the unrelated self is contained by a surrounding object buffered by a protective space. Awareness of his pretense of intersubjective relatedness produced a sense of fraudulence for Mr. L, notably in his marriage, portrayed by him as a kind of parody of a relationship. "I'm pretending to live," he said many times. At other times, however, Mr. L was in the position of the degraded "anal" father—a paternal identification—which could also serve as a bulwark against mother's engulfment, even if putting him in a humiliating posture.

In Ms. G's history, her mother was depicted as oblivious and absent, rather than potentially engulfing, although her fantasy of being used as a masturbatory object had similarities to Mr. L's accounts of his behavior around his mother. I wondered whether her fantasy wasn't constructed in part to provide a connection to a truly uninvolved mother. From this perspective, the sexuality may have been an attempt to inject vitality into an otherwise lifeless relationship (I believe that this would be a correct Kohutian interpretation). Faced with an affective emptiness, perhaps only sadomasochistic enactment offered a simulacrum of aliveness and coherence. Her father, on the other hand, did seem to have a covert desire to use her for narcissistic (autoerotic) purposes, through behaviors that violated his symbolic paternal role. As already noted, prior to analysis, she had abandoned her career and artistic pursuits and further pushed away her husband, focusing exclusively on her young child as giving her life a purpose. We might hypothesize that she was struggling to create basic trust from whole cloth by devotion to her maternal role.

Experiencing the enormous vulnerability of these analysands to any but the most empathic or mirroring responses early in their treatment, I was able to appreciate once again the relevance of Kohut's selfobject concept. For a lengthy period, we remained within this framework, without much possibility for other types of intervention. With time, however, they began to express more safety and comfort in the treatment situation, feeling contained and, to an extent, understood. In retrospect, my holding of painful past memories and my validations of the failure of parental responses to their developmental needs could be viewed as supplying the symbolic *points de capiton* to which I referred earlier. As a witness to things that really happened to them and which exceeded bounds of culturally accepted laws of parental function, I could represent the paternal role (the symbolic function) as a "third." That is, their experiences were not simply subjective constructions or fantasies carrying irrational demands for gratification and denials of parts of themselves (no doubt, such motivations were also present), but dramatized the real absence of a needed presence and a concomitant failure of internalization. The needs of the child for a developmentally necessary parental response are enshrined in common cultural narratives and in ideals (of parenting) that the therapist in a symbolic role inevitably represents.

To lend support to this perspective, in both cases I was soon made aware of the appearance of an idealizing transference that for a time made the treatment a central focus of their lives. Kohut, I suspect, would have interpreted these idealizations as a natural progression from the predominately mirroring transferences that (not without difficulty) had previously been established. This new development also seemed based, at least in part, on preexisting idealized views of psychoanalysis. Mr. L, I later learned, had developed a teenage appreciation for Freud, whom he saw as exposing all the hypocrisy and corruption of the religious and cultural institutions he had come to detest. Similarly, Ms. G recalled that an admired aunt and uncle who had very little tolerance for her parents had made positive comments about psychoanalysis during their infrequent visits. The seeming normality of these relatives was connected in her mind with their interest in analytic ideas, which made them, she said, more human than her rigid parents. Although these idealizations had selfobject qualities (e.g., support of a grandiose self by association with an idealized psychoanalysis), the dominant theme of this phase of the treatment was not grandiosity but a struggle to find people or institutions sufficiently reliable to sustain meaning and value. I suggest that both analysands may have been seeking to reestablish a link to symbolic ideals that had been damaged much earlier in their lives.

The fate of the phase of renewed searching for reliable and worthy objects in the treatment, itself an achievement in the analysis of severely traumatized patients, may depend upon the differentiation of a symbolic transference from the simple idealization of the analyst as a magical figure (the imaginary transference). That is, the analyst may stand in for ideals as symbolic Other without pretending to incarnate them (for instance, in her own narcissistic fantasy) and thereby falling into the countertransference error of perpetuating a grandiose, ideal ego in the mirror. The analyst, if he or she practices correctly, does not simply present his or her own identity and values for mirroring, but holds the place of the Other, that is, of the larger symbolic framework, which is the ground of subjectivity. Just as parents assume symbolic roles that transcend their individual qualities, there is a global structure of signification standing behind each particular analyst who represents those wider functions of the Other in the symbolic transference. These include the rules of secondary process logic, personal boundaries, and recognition of differences of gender and generation that provide a matrix upon which unique historical and biological variables play out. Lacan regarded the analyst as the vehicle for the patient's reengagement in "the universal discourse" of intersubjective speech into which he or she must insert himself or herself to find a place as subject. Kohut saw the importance of idealization genetically as a stage in this process of organizing a "self" that needed to be relived in the transference. Clearly it is crucial how the analyst handles an idealizing transference—not to reject or interpret it away, nor to collude unconsciously with it. Both errors may occur in the course of treatment and are usually apparent only retrospectively, when they can, with good fortune, be interpreted.

An important aspect of idealization is the growth of trust in the analyst, who experiences a greater sense of freedom to express

himself or herself as his or her interventions begin to be heard as
well-intentioned and constructive. Trust develops within the transference if the analyst does not exploit her role, although, of course—
as clinicians have learned from years of experience—there will be
lapses and "enactments" in which past disappointments are repeated in modified forms. Subsequent working through of betray-
als of trust may then lead to a revival or refinding of values and
ideals, often personified, as in the example of Freud for Mr. L. The
ideals, one might say, were always already there within the symbolic (cultural) universe, which contains vocabularies representing
the possibilities for human experience (qualities of mothering, for
instance) and representations of affective response (depictions of
loving behavior). These might exist as formal narratives like legends or myths, as ideal types, or as familiar scenes portraying character that enter into the consolidation of the ego ideal. To a great
extent, the symbolic function must operate through a set of stories
and traditions that circulate in the cultural discourse as a reservoir
of common knowledge. These provide a stock of relational models
against which the subject can measure and judge his own personal
situation and through which his private feelings can be communicated to others who share these narratives. From this perspective,
the vocabulary for complex affects, beyond simple discharge or
display phenomena, is regulated by a symbolic function that defines the cultural sense of emotions and thereby permits a coherent
discourse. To again cite Lutz (1988): "Emotion is about deep commitments to particular other persons and to seeing events in certain ways" (p. 216).

Mr. L saw the major events of his life in drastic terms with a
sense of betrayal, humiliation, and rage that seemed to pass indis-
tinguishably from his parent's experiences as deracinated Holocaust survivors to his own childhood. Their torments merged in
the retelling with his own experiences of a bitter and depressed
mother and a defeated, passive father, as well as of his confining
religious life in the ultraorthodox school. His mother's repetitious
stories of atrocities and displays of books and drawings from the
ghetto were constant presences in his life. It seems likely that her
traumatic past had impaired her capacity to sustain a symbolic
maternal role (she apparently had no real faith, nor much remaining
"basic trust," nor meaningful ideals for herself), just as the father

seemed to abdicate his. Here we could speak clearly of transmission of trauma. In Ms. G's history, the cultural context was a less obvious factor, although we knew that the paternal grandmother had been quite disturbed, and there was a sense of hiding secrets to protect social appearances. Yet her sense of betrayal was equally powerful, as a result of the father's sadistic practices and mother's noninvolvement. Speaking directly about what was actually occurring in their lives was almost unknown in the two households, a commonly reported feature of families of patients suffering traumatic childhoods. Meyerson (1991) emphasized this linguistic deficiency in his papers on childhood dialogues. He stressed that the ability to use traditional analysis depended on the early experience of speaking about emotionally significant events with parents. With patients who have lacked such opportunities, reliving and reenactment are the order of the day. The analyst's task is then to help them move beyond defensive mirroring and idealization to a broader symbolic understanding of the elements in play in their specific histories.

Having experienced elsewhere the impasse that can arise in a static mirroring transference, I tried to remain alert to this potentiality with Mr. L and Ms. G and be attentive to any indications of an acceptance of idealization with grandiose or magical qualities. As a general principle of technique, it is important to maintain a position that is at once attentive to other messages than those contained in the imaginary discourse directed at the selfobject and, at the same time, remains sufficiently flexible and empathic not to lose contact with the patient. While attempting to maintain this rhythm of responsiveness to unconscious communications in counterpart to participation in the imaginary role, the analyst is likely to disappoint at some time, and a reaction of narcissistic rage may then ensue. In such situations, the patient has experienced a failure of attunement with a preferred self-image or self-state, and this loss of the mirror threatens his sense of cohesion. Earlier, I emphasized the dangers of slipping into a subtly sadomasochistic enactment by which the patient may attempt to avoid this risk of fragmentation. Certainly there are mutual elements in all enactments and, in this case, I have always felt that there must be some, at least transitory sharing of the threat by both analyst and patient. Something from the side of the analyst that has entered into the selfobject transference can also become destabilized as the mirror relation breaks down. At such moments, enactments can erupt around seemingly mild exchanges that may take on enormous significance for the analysand.

On one occasion, Mr. L, arriving at the wrong time for his appointment, knocked impatiently at my office door. He perceived my disconcerted reaction as one of disdainful rejection. At the same time, he was bringing a book that he thought would interest me, thrusting it forward in the doorway as he realized I was with another patient. I was left with feelings of intrusion, combined with a kind of excitement and annoyance, as well as a strange sense of loss around the unknown book, now withheld, which had been proferred. Mr. L felt humiliated and subsequently expressed outrage and a sense of betrayal. When I commented on my sense of intrusion during the session and linked it with the larger theme of similar interactions of this kind in the past, both within and outside of psychoanalysis, he became reflective and sad. He said that he had wanted to share something important he believed I would appreciate and to gain reassurance that I was "really there" with him, standing for "something real," not simply acting as the vehicle for another humiliation. This by now familiar scenario of object seeking derailed by anal fantasies (being repudiated as an "undesirable shit") brought into the foreground Mr. L's wish for a "real" and trustworthy connection, succumbing once again to the repetition compulsion. Of course, I had to acknowledge that in my annoyance at his intrusion (and from deeper reactions of which I was finally becoming aware), I had certainly humiliated him. There was no mistaking my part in the sequence, and this admission seemed to bring tremendous relief to Mr. L. As is typical after such exchanges, he was now free to explore his own contribution to the incident, which he could readily see. Through offering me the book, he had created a kind of test situation, which had a high probability of failure, but succeeded in its true goal of bringing the issue of betrayal squarely into the analysis. My recognition of the impact of my reaction at the door helped frame his question of trustworthiness and the "real engagement" he sought, as well as clarifying the childhood traumatic situation for him.

In retrospect (in the *après-coup*), I could now understand the early explosive phase of the analysis as an analogous repetition of trauma. It seemed to me that in my earlier silent struggle with feelings of hatred, as though personally assaulted by Mr. L's nihilistic attacks, I had been unable to respond sufficiently to his extreme distress, perhaps reliving with him an early maternal failure. I found Ferenczi's (1933) moving description of the traumatic effect of a "confusion of tongues" quite helpful in this regard, in the sense that the analyst's failure to respond at the level of the patient's demand can repeat an earlier traumatic situation. Mr. L had been speaking in terms of his early reactions of fear and danger to the transmitted parental traumas, while I was hearing the violent rantings of a neo-Nazi thug. I hypothesize that my interventions at the time, along the lines of an attempt to demarcate past reality from the present, may have been barely enough to hold him in the analysis.

The issue of "reality" arises frequently with these vulnerable patients, who seek a new and not artificial relationship but who have trouble with the dangerous otherness of the object. Of course there were many possible implications of the book incident with Mr. L, of which I would highlight the symbolic failure of his father to pass on a symbolic heritage of Judaism or simply to sustain the paternal function in the transference (the book was, in fact, a biography of Freud). The performative offer of the text suggests an actualized fantasy of Freud occupying the vacated space of the ego ideal, as well as an attempt to install a circuit of reciprocity in which he might learn the nature of his desire from me (my analytic notebook seemed implicated). There was also a reference to his childhood history of anal humiliations in family exchanges (around cleanliness, odors, and bathroom intrusions), about which he had spoken many times. As a boy, Mr. L had been aware of thinking his parents had motives for such behavior that were hypocritically disguised or secret—mother wishing to humiliate him, for example. The book in this respect was a signifier, a metonymic junction of different chains of associations leading in many directions. On yet another level, the book as a concrete link between our outstretched hands suggests the concept of the *objet petit a* of Lacan, the fantasmic lost hyphen connecting and uniting the subject to the Other. In this sense, it could carry a part-object (fecal) meaning of a forbidden enjoyment associated with the object. For all these reasons, Mr. L's expressed wish for a new and authentic friendship was constrained and ultimately undermined by disavowed fantasies that touched the core of his psychic life.

Pressure on the analyst to express what she "really" thinks or to "be real" usually carries the hope for a more authentic relationship, even though it may feel controlling to the analyst or like a misguided effort to actualize a fantasy of an ideal (impossible) situation. Ms. G also spoke about her desire to make her treatment "real" (as opposed to her sense of the "phoniness" of most professional roles and the artificial flavor of interactions in her family). It was easier for her to expose hypocrisy or pretense than to reflect on what she was truly seeking through the set of wishful fantasies she attempted to impose upon me. Usually, analysts attempt to explore this kind of demand, hoping to maintain the field of desire and engagement open, without rejection or undue frustration to the patient. Ferenczi emphasized that analysts who behave in an excessively "clinical" or detached manner may retraumatize a vulnerable patient in urgent need of more frankness and emotional contact. I knew from the beginning that I had to take Ms. G's concerns about "being real" to heart and, hoping to learn more about what was going on, encouraged her to convey her impressions of my behavior and demeanor (which, of course, did not seem so artificial to me). At the same time, I tried my best to remain within the rhythm of movement just suggested and to support the "analytic third," by asking her to reflect on what she was asking of me.

Inevitably, there was a similar enactment with Ms. G that proved important for her analysis. At a certain point, she began to display all the appearances of a negative therapeutic reaction, becoming more hopeless and suicidal with each passing week, without any obvious explanation for her downward spiral. I was very concerned, but also frustrated and impatient, as though it were almost a willful refusal on her part to improve (I was aware of this attitude or my part). Uncertain about what was going on and alarmed by her deepening depression, I decided to raise the suggestion of consultation with a psychopharmacologist. Ms. G was quite outraged, leaving the session early. The following day, she interpreted to me that I was now behaving like her mother, who in her preoccupation with her daughter's physical appearance had sent her to a diet doctor after an adolescent suicidal gesture (the mother believed that her weight was the issue). My proposal of a consultation was thus another betrayal of trust, which we were fortunately now able to reconstruct. My fantasy that she could will herself to recover and use her talent to create a better life for herself proved to be part of this complex reenactment. I, like her mother, expected

Ms. G to actualize my (objectifying) image of her as an attractive, talented woman (daughter). Her deepening depression may have been a reaction to finding herself once again, in her analysis, in prey of the other's desire.

As Ms. G and Mr. L were gradually able to gain more distance from their painful memories after many years of work, they became more able to speak thoughtfully about their experiences without recourse to action or emotional explosions. Slowly, space began to clear for the symbolization of these intolerable states. I saw such changes as a result of a lessened need to rely on the mirror and of the reconstitution of a symbolic space, which opened up possibilities for creative elaboration of affects, now connected to formerly disavowed aspects of their own fears and desires and to a richer understanding of the behaviors of others. Instead of a repetitive fixation around specific traumatic memories and the stereotyped roles associated with them—of which I have highlighted those of victim and persecutor—they could begin to entertain other possibilities for relationships. They seemed freer to undertake a productive reevaluation of the past, notably of transgenerational patterns and continuities that had undoubtedly shaped the early years of their lives (they also accorded me more freedom to explore this history with them). Mr. L, for example, obtained information about his grandparents and great grandparents and contacted other Jewish natives of his country of birth. He also took an interest in the histories of other traumatized peoples. Gradually he spoke of his current relationships in more subtle and sensitive ways, including dialogues with a sympathetic rabbi whom he had encountered. This was in contrast to the earlier monotonous invocation of the cruelty and hypocrisy he found in most institutions. His descriptions now took on a complex moral coloration, with the more primitive inflections assuming a newly humorous form.

Mr. L began to speak about possible explanations for his parents' behavior and for his own emotional states as a young adolescent when his symptoms first appeared, permitting him to locate his perverse fantasies within broader cultural contexts. For instance, his forbidden desires to penetrate, degrade, and dominate, along with their more deeply unconscious passive counterparts, had been accompanied, to his great shame, by a visual image of a Nazi SS trooper and accompanying notions of virility and strength. He was able to trace some of these images more directly to his mother's stories and to photographs and drawings he had viewed as a boy. Eventually, he could speak about them in terms of his own life history without a disruptive enactment of shame, excitement and rage. The Nazi images seemed to involve a complex fusion of narcissistic rage at numerous deprivations and injuries and of a feeling of dirtiness conveyed by his mother toward him, the messy anal child, and toward Jewish men in general. Her obsessive concerns with cleanliness were close to an open fascination with fecal products, an interest that had found a strange counterpart in her encounters with the German invaders in their polished uniforms and their racist tracts about "vermin," of which she had kept copies. Her deep resentment of a controlling, orthodox father, who had limited her education, made her gravitate toward Czech friends, only to feel deeply betrayed by them during the war years. Mr. L's existence as a subject grew out of this soil, with a kind of fecalization of thought and identity. His later guilt-ridden fantasies, which seemed closely related to his mother's preoccupations, expressed both vengeful wishes toward her and submission to her desires. He attacked her viciously at certain moments, only to turn to identification with her against her father and the Jews. Here we could glimpse a certain fundamental satisfaction (a *jouissance*) in his participation in the maternal discourse, which united them in a scorn for lesser mortals.

As he explored these connections between his relationship to his mother and signifiers of the Nazis, the emotional charge seemed to diminish and the memories and images became a history with sad but logical consequences. Mr. L began to express more affectively modulated concerns, like how to get what he wanted from his life, to deal with his unhappy marriage, and to make his Judaism meaningful. The question of what he could get from me without the reduction to anal incorporation became important, as well as his differentiation from me as someone who did not possess the richness of his Jewish experience, which might after all be worth something. He now saw this cultural tradition as a substantial possession that could be shared with many others. At this moment in the analysis, there was a shift in the transference–countertransference, as I experienced a letting go of his fantasy that I carried the knowledge to restore his lost sense of being alive, which seemed to be returning on its own.

Ms. G had a more uneven course in this regard. Despite considerable work on her tendancy toward a sadomasochistic sexualization of her relationships, there were aspects of the erotic transference that were never adequately resolved. She did, however, initiate some important activities that could be regarded as straightforward sublimations of desires that had previously been expressed mainly through acting out. Her pervasive cynicism, always verging on contempt, gave way to enthusiasm for a new professional career, enabling her to find more satisfaction in life outside analysis. She observed that she saw things less in terms of victims and abusers than as a series of complex circumstances affecting families that might even be approached with cautious hopefulness. With these developments and the concommitant loosening of the rigid identifications of mirror relations, she demonstrated more freedom to move between different subjective positions. Her associations showed more openness and play, with greater tolerance of separation and "otherness" from her objects, a change that she recounted in her marriage. We could see that a certain fascination and pleasure in teasing, using, and hurting was a substitute for a more reliable connection with people. As the pull toward these destructive interactions diminished, people remarked that she was easier to be with. At the end, a certain equilibrium of affective presence seemed to have been attained.

HAVING A LIFE

I began with a question: How does a person sustain a life and maintain a position as a speaking subject? Although clearly many things were going on in these two long analyses and the results did not indicate that any miracles had transpired, some answers are suggested by the examples of Mr. L and Ms. G. At first, a flow of affect necessary to animate the tension arc of vital speech seemed lacking, and the state of psychic deadness referred to by Green was palpable in their sessions. After this initial lifeless period, the global repression broke down and, in a second phase, powerful manifestations of emotion appeared. At this point, the failure of Kohut's pole of ideals or of a suturing of experience to the symbolic register (to a network of signification), as proposed by Lacan, seemed in question. Affective expression was raw, barely translated from somatic experience into subjective mentalization, apparently reproducing earlier states of helplessness and "subjective annihilation" (Little, 1990), pulling them toward the real of dedifferentiation. At this point, solely enactment of sadomasochistic fantasies seemed to provide coherence by stabilizing images of self and other around these primitive affects. I have discussed this phenomenon in terms of a clinging to an imaginary or mirroring relationship as a solution to the threat of fragmentation, although at some cost.

Trauma appeared to be an important thread in both analyses. I have understood it in terms of parental failures in symbolic holding, which had left these analysands caught between an intrusive overpresence of the object, usurping their subjective space, and an intolerable absence and deadness of the object. I have hypothesized that this oscillation between abuse and abandonment damaged basic trust and thereby interfered with symbolic identification and establishment of an ego ideal. In general, one could hypothesize a vacillation or even the abdication of a symbolic role at crucial times by the parents that, apart from specific destructive acts, produced the trauma. Verbal expression of these experiences of betrayal by parents emerged through analysis of enactments of similar experiences in the transference, reopening issues of trustworthiness and worthy ideals. My unconscious participation in these reenactments, of which I have discussed the book episode for Mr. L and my psychopharm referral for Ms. G, provided a context in which the issue of betrayal of trust could be addressed. The presenting picture of disillusionment, alienation, and cynicism may have been a defensive response to such traumas, conveying in the transference both an appeal and an attack on the ego ideal. Behind this presentation, a fantasy structure of a kind of enjoyment and satisfaction (*jouissance*) in an impossible joining the too absent or too present object could be discerned.

Placing the question of sustaining a sense of aliveness in Lacanian terms, I highlighted the embeddedness of my analysands in two forms of imaginary discourse, one expressing a "negative hallucination of self," the other adhering to objectified images of self as victim. In the absence of a symbolic link to social narratives, values, and principles, they were unable to pursue desire through fuller speech and through more reciprocal intersubjective relations. I have situated the analytic work (selectively, of course) within the framework of reconstitution of the functions of an ego ideal or of reestablishment of links to the "pole of values" within the symbolic order, which allow for variegated affective narratives. Both analysands were increasingly able to carry their desires, hatreds, and fears into dialogue with others, perhaps with a link to the Other in Lacanian terms (entering into the universal discourse instead of captation by images). First, there was an expanded ability to interact in the analysis and to consider what was being said by me without the exquisite sensitivity to disconfirmation in the mirror. Gradually there was increased interchange with others, without loss of the vital (and painful) content of their histories. In this way, affect as a "signifier of the flesh" could fuel a reestablished tension arc, binding private self experience to the cultural symbols that alone can provide a symbolic anchoring for the fragmented self.

5

The Objet Petit a

It is a question of this privileged object . . . around which the drive moves, of that object that arises in a bump, like the wooden darning egg in the material which, in analysis, you are darning—the objet a.
—JACQUES LACAN

IN CHAPTER 4, I MADE BRIEF REFERENCE TO THE CONCEPT OF THE *OBJET petit a* (object small a) in describing the fantasy structure underlying important enactments. Here, I further develop this idea in relation to the theme of sustaining a subjective identity—of having a separate life. Like many of Lacan's concepts, the *objet petit a* is elusive in its meaning and referent and seems to take on different functions over the course of his work. My purpose is not to attempt to resolve or explicate these difficulties through a comprehensive account of Lacanian theory but rather to explore whether this notion in some of the ways it has been understood can be applied advantageously to clinical problems and practice. In its most common definition, the *objet petit a* represents a quasimathematical symbol for a hypothetical or virtual construct, namely the ephemeral, unlocalizable something in the object that makes it especially desirable. Lacan speaks of it as the "cause" of the subject's desire. In this sense, it does not refer to some hitherto unknown psychic function discovered by Lacan (although he considered it his only new contribution to Freud's work), but simply fills in a logically necessary step in the subject's response to his objects.

However one evaluates Lacan's argumentation or methods of reasoning in the seminars (at times they are infuriating), his concept

103

of desire, structured around a hypothetical cause of desire, offers a way of understanding common clinical phenomena. As Van Haute (2002) aptly remarked, a purely object-centered conception of desire (based on attributes of the desired object) would mean that many partners possessing these features would be equally interchangeable. Likewise, if desire were simply a matter of instinctual drives, one passionate interest could easily substitute for another. Because sexual choice is so variable in human beings, Freud saw fit to lay his emphasis on a certain mobility of libidinal drive energy, but it seems just as useful to focus on the nature of the underlying fantasy structure, which selects the object as the key to this problem. The concept of the *objet petit a* describes this idiosyncratic unconscious source of subjective motivation that, Lacan insists, has no realizable aim or goal, analogous to Freud's characterization of childhood sexuality. Lacan argued that aims and goals, even in adult sexual behavior, are inadequate to satisfy desire, a leftover part of which always remains operative. Although the fantasy driving desire is unconscious and unrelated to symbolic reality, it can be attached to concrete objectives like sexual pleasure and social and material accomplishments, which can be pursued and enjoyed within the limitations of the pleasure and reality principles. Because of these constraints of the symbolic order, these goals always fall short of providing the total satisfaction or *jouissance* sought by the fantasy, leaving a constant remainder of unsatisfied desire as an intrinsic aspect of the human condition. Under some circumstances, however, the insistent pressure of desire can be short-circuited into inhibitions, actions, or symptom formation, which interfere with the constant investments that make living pleasurable.

Many persons seeking psychotherapy, as we saw in the histories of Mr. L and Ms. G, lack access to desire and report feeling flat, dull, and not fully alive. Not being able to feel love is a common complaint. On the other hand, it should be obvious that actual loving relationships between partners cannot be explained by an abstract concept like the *objet petit a* any more than by the Freudian notion of libido. Both terms are basically metapsychological constructs attempting to bridge the impossible gap between biological and psychological existence. For Lacan, as we have seen, subjective experience in man is dependent entirely on language. For him, the capacity to use symbols, including identifying pronouns, and the ability to employ proper names is what makes us human. This is what he means when he repeats in many ways that the subject is an effect of the signifier. There is thus a break from the biological real created by the symbolic order, which in a way captures and restructures the organic basis of life. The body, for example, is conceptualized and organized by labels and categories that stand in the way of any unmediated experience of its reality. As Erik Erikson wisely theorized, the body is carved up into erogenous zones that have social and personal significance beyond simple sensitivity to stimulation. Our experience is always filtered through language and the spread of meanings through associations. As the philosopher Hillary Putnam (1981) has stated, we have no access to such a thing as a language independent reality, or, in Lacan's (1972–1973) idiom, there is "no prediscursive reality" (p. 72).

On the other hand, the symbolic order always falls short of totally capturing lived experience, inevitably excluding a part of the real in which we are rooted. This insufficiency is attributable to the very nature of symbols, which are structured inherently around missing or absent objects. A symbol, after all, represents an absent object or, put differently, signifies an abstract concept, and language can only allude to a concrete external referent without totally capturing it. For Lacan, the inability of the symbolic to totally encompass its referents or to represent fully what has been lost creates a constant gradient of desire, a perpetual reaching out for the pure reality beyond representation. In the Lacanian formula, desire "insists" in the signifying chain, with its Bellowesque[1] "I want, I want" pushing us unceasingly toward dimly perceived goals and the deferred promise of complete satisfaction. Because such goals are impossible to realize, we substitute fantasies of sexual, romantic, narcissistic, or material accomplishment, which stitch desire to the fabric of social reality. We convince ourselves (or are manipulated to believe[2]) that we will be satisfied by realizing these ends. Desire thus becomes "libidinized" and diverted to existing symbolic objects. Such is the Lacanian vision of the world.

Something interferes with this process of desiring for many people, or, it might be more accurate to say, something is always

---

[1]Referring to the unquenchable desire of the hero of Saul Bellow's (1953) novel, *The Adventures of Augie March.*

[2]This intuitive exploitation of unconscious desire by advertising that alludes to "more" or "extra" in a product is critiqued by Zizek (1989) in his analysis of the modern capitalist state.

interfering with desire for everyone. Desire, after all, can be un-comfortable, even dangerous, so that short-circuiting its insistent flow into symptoms is a universal human propensity. In order to understand this twist in the Lacanian story, we need to introduce his important notion of *jouissance* (literally, "enjoyment"), men-tioned earlier in relation to a "beyond" of the pleasure principle. *Jouissance* refers basically to the full satisfaction that we uncon-sciously pursue. Because such satisfaction is by the nature of our symbolic existence impossible, attempts to approach it breach the boundary of the symbolic and the limits of the pleasure principle, which is constrained by what we can "enjoy" (without unpleasure or harm) in the world of symbolic reality. *Jouissance* is therefore "beyond the pleasure principle" and definitely not conventionally "enjoyable." Rather, it has a deadly aspect in that it operates without regard for the welfare of the subject, including her personal mean-ing, pleasures, and symbolic identity, and when approached is ac-companied by pain and distress. This creates a tension in Lacanian theory between *desire*, the property uniquely belonging to human subjects, who live "suspended" from the symbolic order by signifiers (by abstract indications of meanings, identifying marks, and social coordinates—the ensemble of social rules and beliefs), and *jouissance*, the unconscious desubjectifying pull away from the sym-bolic order. Lacan's subject is thus split in her very essence by an unconscious that obeys its own rules, alien to the rational order of conscious experience, and is condemned to a state of dissatisfaction.

Lacan raises the question of what it is about an object that gives it (a person, idea, or physical thing) the mysterious property of evoking intense desire. For example, let us take the case of an unknown man who is attractive to a woman. Initially, her interest might be aroused by his conformity to social criteria of physical beauty, by a pleasing manner of speaking, an aura of wealth and power, unusual intelligence, and so forth. Some kind of imaginary screening process is no doubt at work, along with symbolic factors that render the man a potentially eligible partner. If nothing hap-pens to negate this initial impression, the woman may experience desire for the man, which might even become intense very quickly. She might be uncomfortable with this feeling and fend it off, not being sure about the person or even in what her interest actually consisted. The feeling of desire itself might be pleasant or disturbing to her; she could try to ignore it or talk herself out of it, although this seems difficult for most people. Supposing everything works in favor of the attraction and she pursues her inclinations to enter into a romantic relationship, how might she explain her choice to friends or family? Certainly she cannot claim that she is falling in love with this man for his wonderful personality, his aura of success, or his brilliance without sounding defensive or disingenuous. Although such locutions are sometimes employed by people, they are usually understood either as euphemisms for conveying high regard and appreciation or else as incomplete, evasive answers that disguise deeper feelings. After all, the woman probably has met other handsome, smart, pleasant men before without falling in love. Surely this one is not the first to come along, and, even if he were, the glamor attached to his novelty would rapidly wear thin. The point is that listing all the fine or materially impressive qualities of the love object does not satisfactorily explain why that particular person is so special or has aroused the unique feeling of desire with which almost everyone is familiar (which is why our hypothetical woman is not likely to be asked such a naive question).

No one, after all, is obliged to account for why he or she loves anything or anybody, and the same goes, of course, for other kinds of passionate interest—Beethoven sonatas, Hitchcock films, a sport—that some people pursue at great cost and with enormous devotion. In general, this type of powerful emotional imperative that seizes us all is accepted as part of the human condition, provided that the response remains within the bounds of symbolic reality, which means that the subject accepts responsibility for his choice as a personal construction and respects the autonomy of the object and her own place in the social network. When it comes to relationships between people, passion is valued, but unwelcome pursuit is disapproved of. Stalking violates the law. We could say that although a beloved person represents in part, in Winnicott's (1953) terms, a subjective object, "created" by the lover, he also possesses independent reality as another subject. This distinction is less clear in the case of purely symbolic or inanimate objects, which are more analogous to Winnicott's transitional object. In the latter case, we do not pose the question of whether the intense feeling for a special object being pursued is "real" or entirely created by the subject. Winnicott observes that the unquestioned illusion of a unique transitional object evolves over time into the contents of a shared cultural space that provides constraints and structure to what might otherwise be purely idiosyncratic choices. This realistic anchoring of desire is most obvious in the case of the love object. Here is the point where narcissism as a motivation for object choice is limited by one's place in a symbolic and intersubjective field. Although the choice of another person as a love object may similarly be taken as "real" by the subject, as if that special object alone could fulfill his or her desire (it is more accurately an entirely imaginary construction of the subject), there is a boundary of symbolic reality that may not be crossed without agreement of the other. That is, a man must accept that his fantasies of love and passion are his own invention and that, even when such fantasies and passions seem mutually shared, there remains a gap between these private feelings and the reality of the other person. One might even propose that acknowledgment of this discrepancy is a necessary step for symbolic love to proceed.[3] If this boundary is crossed and the fantasy object of desire is taken as congruent with the real object, as though the other could totally satisfy the fantasy, the subject enters the realm of perversion or psychosis.

An illustration of this distinction is provided in Almodovar's film, "Talk to Her" (*Hable con Ella*). In the film, two men are in love with comatose women and develop a friendship based on this identification, but there the similarity ends. Marco, the more experienced, tragic figure, is grief-stricken over the fatal wounding of his lover, a female toreador, only to learn that she had decided to return to her former partner just before her accident. His choice of object, occurring when she was in good health, was typically neurotic and oedipal—he rescued her in a futile repetition of an earlier lost love. His counterpart, Benigno, while also falling in love with a normal woman, Alicia, has never actually known her, only gazed at her from a window—a purely imaginary relationship that followed the loss of his mother, who was his sole previous object. Benigno becomes Alicia's nurse after an accident has left her too in a coma, and she becomes the passion of his existence, to the point

---

[3]Lacan (1972–1973) emphasized the necessary failure of the sexual relationship to provide the satisfaction desired. "Isn't it owing only to the affect that results from this gap that something is encountered? . . . The substitution by the path of existence not of the sexual relationship but of the unconscious . . . which constitutes the destiny as well as the drama of love" (p. 145). In other words, love rises beyond the level of a narcissistic (sexual) fantasy through the encounter of two speaking beings.

of his confiding to Marco that he wants to marry her. Marco is appalled, but this scene of confrontation is only a prelude to the more shocking revelation that Benigno, after viewing a silent science fiction film in which a miniaturized man enters the vagina of his beloved and joins her body, has impregnated Alicia. The consequences for him, of course, are drastic, and he eventually dies in a failed attempt to join her in her unconscious state by taking an overdose.

Benigno illustrates certain aspects of the *objet petit a* to which we will return, notably its relation to an "enjoyment" (*jouissance*) beyond the pleasure principle that is linked to the register of the real in Lacan. His talking about marriage to Marco could be considered an acting-out, in Lacanian terms, because it confronts his friend with a message about the nature of his interest in Alicia. It draws attention to the external presence or imaginary actualization of the *objet petit a* in an insistent form. Something in Alicia that has nothing to do with her individual personality or unique personal life has drawn Benigno. No doubt this desire has at first attached itself to a sexual fantasy, as we can see in his sensual attention to the care of her skin earlier in the film. According to Lacan, there is a further possible step, which he calls *passage à l'acte* (passing to action or "acting out"), in which the subject identifies with and moves to join the *objet petit a*.[4] This occurs when he attempts to move beyond the fantasy of a forbidden pleasure toward a total enjoyment of *jouissance*, which in Benigno's case seems to involve merger or a return to the womb as a "presubject." Here his life is literally placed in danger by a desire to go "beyond the pleasure principle" of ordinary sexuality.

Benigno's story underlines the impossible nature of the *objet petit a* (unsymbolizable and unimaginable), its unattainability and pure virtuality, as something that "exists" in the object only by inference. It is thus unassimilable to a bodily pleasure that could be obtained or represented in the symbolic dimension. We could say that Benigno wanted something from Alicia that could not be put into words. Subtracting all the various sexual and romantic wishes he might have expressed still leaves a remainder, the unknown residue that is the "true" cause of desire. To describe it,

---

[4]Lacan discussed this difference in his exceptionally difficult seminar on anxiety (1962–1963). Harari (2001) offers a reasonably lucid explication of this seminar.

Lacan (1960–1961) used the metaphor of the *algama*, the hidden treasure or small deity that Socrates evoked in Plato's *Symposium,* whose theme is precisely the definition of the ingredient making the beloved desirable to the lover. The *objet petit a*, of course, is a creation of the subject. It is Benigno's *objet petit a* that he thinks he has found in his beloved (but perhaps this person does unwittingly carry a signifier of this treasure object, some feature that is linked to an unconscious fantasy of the *object petit a*). It is something in Alicia that is more than her, but that she supports.

In Kundera's (1984) novel, *The Unbearable Lightness of Being*, the author refers to a character's love for the woman inside his wife, for he truly cannot stand her actual personality and appearance. Kundera asks who is this hidden woman and interprets that it is his mother. For Lacan, the answer is a deeper one that refers neither to the imago or fantasy of the mother "herself," which might be "cathected" in Freudian terms (which seems to be Kundera's take on Franz's devotion to Marie-Claude), nor to part of a more abstract relational unit in a self- psychological sense, but rather to a nonimaged, nonsymbolized "remainder" of his mother that has been carried from his infancy and childhood, long after the subject has come to see her as a separate adult. With Klein, perhaps, Lacan would not see this enduring desire of Kundera's character as directed toward the whole object, but to a part, perhaps like a part-object that remains as a trace of the imaginary link between his body and his mother's. Yet this "object" is not a body part but a virtual object of a fantasy established retrospectively, after the child has assumed his differential position in the social order. This again is the *objet petit a*, to which Lacan in either a stroke of genius or sophistry gave his quasialgebraic nomenclature, placing it at the heart of human motivation (the pursuit of non-utilitarian, irrational, even nonlibidinal desires).

The references to Klein's notion of a part-object and to Winnicott's transitional object seem to locate the *objet petit a* in a developmental context, and, at times, Lacan does give the impression of wanting to identify it as a vestige of completion or full connection with the earliest object that will be lost, the breast. Of course, Lacan everywhere eschews developmental references, which he sees as a form of psychologizing or biologizing of a maturational process that does not exist as such. For him, the so-called early stages (oral, anal, phallic) only take their significance retroactively, via the effect of castration. Castration was conceived by him as the "presence" of a lack or of an inherent incompleteness in the human subject that produces a sequence of virtual *objets petit a*: the breast, feces, the gaze, and the voice. Lacan (1972–1973) spells this out in his discussion of envy in Seminar XX, where he once again recounts the scene described by Augustine of the pale and envious child observing his nursing sibling. Here, he says that for this child the baby at the breast has the *a*, referring to "the kernel of what I called Ding (the thing)"[5] (p. 100).

Lacan's fascination with the retroactive, nonchronologic moment of psychic birth through the agency of the signifier (the cut made by a system of differences into the unity of the real) had a metaphorical enactment in the story of his purchase of Courbet's famed painting, "*L'Origine du Monde*" (The Origin of the World), recounted by Roudinesco (1993). It is a portrayal of a nude woman's torso, exposing the genitals in what remains a shockingly realistic manner, which had been commissioned from Courbet for private viewing by a Turkish diplomat in 1866. Following in this tradition, Lacan kept the picture concealed behind a special cover painted by another artist. Courbet also painted a number of scenes around the same year depicting the subterranean source of the river Loue, in one of which the solitary figure of a fisherman seems to be casting his rod into the darkness of an enormous cave mouth from which the river emerges. These images evoke fascination and horror that have been commented upon by many art historians.[6] The retroactive wish to return to the womb as an aftereffect of symbolic castration is mediated by the *objet petit a*. In this fantasy, rejoining the body of the mother will provide *jouissance*, total pleasure, and Lacan hypothesized that the child attributes this same desire to the mother.

For Lacan (1962–1963), the conception of an engulfing, reabsorbing mother—a "crocodile mother"—played an important part in his later theories of anxiety. He proposed that the subject is drawn to participate in the supposed "*jouissance* of the Other,"

---

[5]*Das Ding* as a philosophic concept carries a lot of freight, pointing to the real but unknowable object apart from our limited capacity to perceive and conceive it, as developed by Kant. Freud picked up this notion when he spoke of the unconscious as similarly unknowable, and Lacan developed it much further, using *Das Ding* as a metaphor for the preobjectal mother.

[6]An excellent review of this history is provided by Barzilai (1999).

meaning the ultimate enjoyment that belongs in fantasy to the mother. The *objet petit a*, in a sense, functions protectively as an intermediary target of desire that indicates a lack in the Other (the virtual part-object or link with the presymbolized mother that has fallen away with primal separation).[7] It thereby represents and confirms the occurrence of separation and protects against a wish for fusion.

One wonders to what extent Almadovar was explicitly restaging this fantasy of *jouissance* in his silent film within a film, in which a woman scientist discovers her miniature former lover, who has drunk her weight loss potion and shrunk to Tom Thumb size. Clearly enchanted, she brings him to her home, where he seizes the opportunity to explore her sleeping body, ultimately standing before a huge vaginal opening into which he will plunge, recalling Courbet's tiny angler before the gaping source of the Loue.[8] Lacan would say that it is her *jouissance* which the little man seeks to participate in or produce, a point echoed by Benigno's incredible devotion to the unconscious Alicia, whom he wants to join beyond any possible symbolic, intersubjective relationship in a total union. For the neurotic person, to the contrary, *jouissance* is clearly barred, as the symbolic order does not include the possibility of completion or wholeness, but constantly redirects desire within the limits of the pleasure principle.

Clinical complaints of apathy, lack of motivation, loss of sexual interest, or inability to love may all be related to a difficulty in assuming one's desire as a subject or as agent of this desire. At one level of meaning, this difficulty implies a failure to pass through an oedipal position, which involves acceptance of loss and separateness, a capacity to tolerate guilt for transgressive wishes, and man-

[7]Harari (2001) presents one of Lacan's formulae for the *objet petit a* as: O (the mother in the first instance) minus S (the incipient subject) equals a. The entire thrust of Lacan's argument is toward a structure underlying the phenomenology of separation, much like Piaget's was toward the mathematical rules structuring the stages of reasoning. This helps explain why his text is so abstract and seems to ignore the actual experience of the child, as infant researchers, for example, attempt to reconstruct it. In my view, because the mathematics proposed by Lacan has in nearly every instance been shown to be fallacious or virtually meaningless (see Sokol and Bricmont, 1997), we need to rethink his hypotheses in relation to clinical and empirical psychoanalytic research.
[8]Freud's (1900) horrifying vision of Irma's oral cavity in his famous dream specimen may be another version of this compelling fantasy.

agement of fears of retaliation or punishment. In the Lacanian framework, assumption of desire presupposes symbolic castration, which means renouncing identification with an ideal ego image (the goal of perfection of an ideal self) and the fantasy of forming a complete unity with the object (of being able to fulfill all the desires of the object). Neither the self nor the object can be complete, and, in the first instance, this lesson is taught by the mother's desire for a third party, usually the father. Lacan's model debiologizes human development by dispensing with a pseudophysiology of libidinal stages and the concrete threat of castration as a motivator. Instead, it emphasizes an anthropological, structural determinant in the social reality of the child's insertion into a network of relationships that sharply limit and define her possibilities (age, gender, birth order, and so forth). Lacan's terms phallus and castration are thus lifted for better or worse out of their customary psychoanalytic context to serve abstract structural functions. He redefined the familiar Freudian castration complex as an imaginary fear based on fantasies of the perfect phallus satisfying the mother, which might be an indication of psychosis for Lacan (which is not to say that neurotic castration fears do not interfere with desire). At the same time, Lacanian theory avoids the post-Freudian danger of a saccharinized family love story in which empathy for the child's irrational and exhibitionistic wishes smooths a path toward joyous initiative. Neither a libidinal, bodily model of development nor one driven by affect and intersubjectivity works for Lacan, and steering clear of these alternatives, which were in the air at the time Lacan worked, provided the novelty and insight as well as the limitations of his conception.

Lacanian theory eschews a developmental model (although I do not believe that, in the end, that model can be successfully ignored) in favor of a nonlinear picture of recursive restructuring upon entry into the symbolic order (which is a post-facto, nonchronological moment). The child's assumption of her place in the symbolic entails a sacrifice of the pre-lapsarian[9] fantasy object of *jouissance* and of total satisfaction in the real, which, however, does not cease to exercise its attraction. In another way, however, this step could be said to create retroactively the lost object as a "beyond" existing outside the fabric of the pleasure principle, a

---

[9]Before the Fall.

remainder of the real precipitated when the symbolic framework congealed around the nascent subject. This remainder of the real, of course, is another definition of the *objet petit a*. In other terms, the ultimate treasure object of our desire is defined as beyond what we can see, know, or symbolize. It can be regarded as an expression of the real (because it has real effects on behavior and even upon the body), but is graspable only in retrospect as what has always eluded our knowledge of ourselves. So we say that our hypothetical lover did not willfully choose her beloved but discovered that choice only after it happened.

THE CASE OF WENDY

At this point, it may be useful to bring in clinical material to explore the application of these concepts. Wendy was a young woman referred to me by a female therapist with whom she had worked for several years on problems of self-esteem, binge eating, and substance abuse. Much progress had been made, but one crucial difficulty had not been resolved. Although desperately hoping to marry and have children, she had never sustained a relationship with a man, having a history of only brief sexual encounters. Over the telephone, she sounded intelligent and thoughtful and spoke with a certain poise. Her therapist had suggested, Wendy informed me, that she might make more progress at this point with a male analyst, and she was eager to try this option.

At our first meeting, however, Wendy arrived in a highly anxious and disorganized state. After the initial formalities, she launched into telling a dream of the previous night that had greatly disturbed her. In the dream, she had come to my office, which turned out to be a large room containing an unmade queen-size bed, where I greeted her in pajamas. The incongruity between office setup and bedroom was troubling to her, but she could not say much about it except that she had felt confused about why she was supposed to be there.

My immediate interpretation of the dream (which I kept to myself) was that her therapist had referred her with the objective of helping her find a man—a sexual love object—and that in her unconscious, she had taken a shortcut and equated that person with me. In other words, I was the object of her desire, but a forbidden, transgressive one as a professional person, paternal symbol, and oedipalized partner to her former therapist. From this perspective, her classic hysterical problem was one of guilt and perhaps fear of retaliation by her mother, on whom she presumably depended consciously or unconsciously. Indeed, she went on to recount a history of a very poor relationship with a volatile mother, whom she portrayed as always critical of everyone. Conversely, she ascribed her progress in the prior treatment to the positive feelings about herself engendered by the warmer and more accepting therapist, as well as to her ability to translate that experience into an improved relationship with her mother. She felt able to understand her mother better and to be more tolerant of her moods, and mother had responded with greater empathy about some of the painful episodes of Wendy's childhood. Also in the picture was a highly idealized father, who was viewed as having been a more involved and, in his way, affectionate parent.

My obvious interpretation of the dream certainly influenced my relationship with Wendy and led me to explore her deep love for her father and the enduring wish to capture more of his attention with diminished shame and guilt. He was a dynamic man who enjoyed outdoor sports, adventure, and discovery of the world, radiating an enthusiasm that attracted many people. Wendy had been his sidekick, tagging along on trips and learning the skills he valued so that she could keep up as she got older, an achievement that had carried over onto her current friendships with men who shared similar active interests. Her mother, needless to say, wanted no part of this type of pastime, but preferred more artistic pursuits, not too subtly disdaining the stereotypic male posture of her husband. Without getting into the details of this part of the treatment, it seemed clear enough that this was not the ideal loving parental couple inspiring normal desires of a child to take the mother's place, but an unhappy situation in which there was not enough love and acceptance to go around. For whatever reasons, there had been a failure of the parents to fulfill their symbolic roles, a blurring of boundaries, and the generation of considerable fantasy of the "she (or he) would love me more if . . ." variety. The familiar clinical reconstruction was one of a depressed child seeking stimulation in a derivative way as a substitute for missing symbolic nourishment.

Over time, I became able to perceive another dynamic in Wendy's relationship with her father, one in which she had occupied an important place in his life. Early in childhood, she had noticed his pride and happiness when impressing friends on their outings and, unconsciously (it seemed implicit, but out of her awareness), she realized that her mother did not provide this mirroring admiration he seemed to crave. Wendy did enjoy their activities, but their entire purpose, she came painfully to realize, had to do with him, who planned, organized, and carried them out, sometimes with her in a purely spectator role. She watched him perform and attended him appreciatively, delighted when his pleasure spilled over onto her in the form of an open smile or affectionate names and jokes, making her feel important. In some of her adult relationships, she had evidenced a similar pattern, attracted to athletic men who were happy to have her company, although rarely bestowing father's special look upon her. These men were frustrating to Wendy because, in the end, she was not important to them, except for brief moments when she might make herself useful to their purposes.

Out of all the complex elements of this analysis, I wish to highlight a question that began to emerge from Wendy's account of these relationships—namely, in its initial version, the query, "What do I have to do to be desired by these guys?" Later it became refined as, "What would *or* does a man want from me?" Of course, for Lacan, this is the fundamental question of the child, often discussed in the form of *che vuoi* posed to the Other. "What is my purpose here? You, the Other, must have some use for me."[10] It is the crucial dynamic that revolves around Lacan's notion of symbolic castration—the incompleteness of the Other and of the self. In her childhood, Wendy had stepped into the role of object of her father's desire, or, more accurately, we could hypothesize that she unwittingly represented the *objet petit a* sought by him in the form of her admiring gaze. She was there in her existence in this unhappy family, finally, for him, attempting to provide an ingredient he sought in his emotional life, hoping, no doubt, that it was her as a person he wanted (that she was truly the object of his desire). When we began to explore what she was seeking from him, however, the picture changed, and we entered a phase of disappointment, hurt, and bitterness. Her father was generous, and

---

[10]". . . all the child's *whys* reveal not so much an avidity for the reason of things as a testing of the adult, a *"Why are you telling me this?"* ever resuscitated from its base, which is the enigma of the adult's desire" (Lacan, 1964, p. 214).

he was fun to be with, but when Wendy had tried to gain his attention about her unhappiness and her struggles to find herself as an
adolescent young woman, he could not remain attentive, minimizing
or papering over the painful issues of her childhood. If she tried to
protest or confront him with her experience, he grew angry, accusing
her of blaming her problems on him or of being too self-indulgent.
In short, speaking of her own desires was out of bounds, seemingly
a threat to his own self-image.

Naturally, this theme emerged in the transference. In truth, it
had been there the first day, had I been able to see it. Wendy's
dream was a way of posing her question, "What is this man going
to want from me?" Frequently, she was surprised that a man would
desire her sexually, as she considered herself unattractive, and the
man, she usually thought, could have more appealing women. At
other times, she simply felt exploited, as she had happened to be
around when the man needed sex, and, for this reason, rarely got
pleasure from the act. Only on a few occasions, when she was
intoxicated and took a more active part, picking up a man (usually
someone who posed no threat of rejection), did she experience or-
gasm. On the other hand, she spoke consistently about enjoying
the experience of being desired by the man (the admired, idealized
object). Somehow this near-perfect being needed her!

The dream staged her perennial confusion about what a man
could possibly be seeking from her; it situated her in the structure
of the other's desire. Her own desires blocked from symbolic elaboration were symptomatically tied to the *jouissance* of symptoms—
eating and substance abuse—which were "pleasurably painful" or
painfully pleasurable, beyond the enjoyment of the pleasure principle and even, in much earlier days, posing a threat to her life. It
was true that she loved her father, was drawn to him despite the
frustrations of their relationship, and, as she said, saw something
in him at his work and in his treatment of her at privileged moments that made him a special person. Sometimes she fleetingly
recaptured this special feeling with one of the men whom she be-
friended. That unique indescribable something was the *objet petit
a*, the cause of her desire, the lost part of herself she sought to
regain in him.

Further developing this formulation, Wendy's effort to please
father and fulfill his desire may have represented an attempt (or
her insistent wish) to identify with the *objet petit a*, which could

fill the lack in him, restoring him as the complete, ideal object she sought. In that way she might realize her desire to participate in the *jouissance* of the Other, a form of denial of separation and loss. Žižek (1989) writes in this context that "the problem for the hysterical subject is that he always needs to have recourse to another subject to organize his desire . . . hysterical desire is the desire of the other" (p. 187). We can see here an acting out, an attempt to actualize a fantasy that was painful to her for many reasons. Certainly it led to constant frustration and disappointment. More important, perhaps, seeking to become the object of her father's desire transgressed the law of the symbolic order and was fundamentally unacceptable, dangerously close to an incestuous love, hence evoking guilt and self-punitive wishes. Beyond this standard oedipal interpretation, however, her fantasy of filling the gap in the other meant throwing herself away as a subject, negating herself as a separate subject.

The imaginary nature of Wendy's identification as the admiring, helpless female, inept on her own and longing to be rescued by a strong generous man, was played out in other relationships, as became clear in the analysis of a series of these liaisons. With these men, she alternated between complaining bitterly of how, in the end, she was only there for them, as the "nothing sidekick" along for the ride, while, conversely, insisting on her love and admiration. Her efforts to become the object of their desires left her in the position of always hoping to be loved by an ideal father who could provide everything she lacked or had lost. Her investment in this ideal ego, an essentially narcissistic position, left her always feeling inadequate and overwhelmed by the unattainability of the men she pursued.

On the other hand, her identification with an invidious but common female stereotype may in some ways have anchored Wendy to the social-symbolic world as a compromise solution to her true subjective dilemma of finding her own desire. That is, through her role as sidekick, she gained the semblance of a "cohesive self," as suggested by a decrease in symptoms of eating or use of drugs during periods when these relationships were most active.

Alongside these "imaginary" relations, there were abundant indications of a complementary *symbolic* identification with her father. For example, in her career and friendships Wendy displayed aspects of the expansive, competent, and adventurous men she admired. She took charge of others easily, could function as a leader when called upon, and many of her friends apparently looked up to her for the strength and assertiveness she could display. Why had this identification not led to a stronger sense of self-esteem and confidence, as one might expect? Her identification with her father was noticed by family members (who said she "took after" him), and this was a positive feature in the eyes of their community, where he was a respected figure. Indeed, I had many occasions to comment upon aspects of her that were similar to admired traits of her father and to wonder why she did not value herself for them. Following Lacan (1960–1961), these features could have functioned as signs, marking the *einziger Zug* of symbolic identification (see footnote 2, chapter 4). Instead, she had turned to self-defeating relationships, which enacted her fantasies of union, and to symptomatic binges, both of which risked evolving, in Lacan's terms, into a *passage à l'acte*, when she had come close at times to a fatal accident or courted suicidal feelings after rejection—in short, a deadly *jouissance*.

In terms of the issue just discussed of the protective nature of the symptom against the pull toward *jouissance*, Lacan placed his emphasis on whether the *objet petit a* was situated externally or was identified with. When the cause of desire is external, it maintains the incompleteness of the subject (symbolic castration), and the condition of metonymic desire can then perpetuate itself in the unending, signifying chain of thoughts and actions. The lack in the subject turns unceasingly toward object-related fantasies expressed symbolically, which is the normal, neurotic state of affairs. The "I want" is never satisfied, always looking for something more, especially so for those whose symbolic links to ideals are weak or who belong to fragmented social settings. In my interpretation, the social context provides the *points de capiton* (in the form of shared narratives, for example) where signifiers of desire can be quilted down to consensual "reality," stabilizing the endless "I want."[11] In

---

[11]In his seminar on the psychoses, Lacan (1955–1956) proposed that a certain minimum number of such points of insertion between the signifier and the signified, halting the perpetual sliding of meaning, was necessary for a subject to personalize (or subjectify) his own discourse. In my view, a similar link with socially given symbols of affective experience is necessary to stabilize a sense of existence and identity.

contrast, imaginary identification attempts to deny lack by pursuing wholeness through symptomatic behavior. At a further stage, Lacan proposed that acting-out (*passage à l'acte*) stages reunion with the lost partial object and hence carries the subject beyond the pleasure principle (to a break with reality and, ultimately, to death, in Benigno's case). We could translate this distinction between imaginary and symbolic identification into the opposition between a narcissistic, private reality that is unbounded and insensitive to the otherness of the object and an intersubjective reality that accepts limitation, lack, and difference.

Although I cannot fully answer the question of why Wendy had remained dominated so long by her imaginary identification (which occurs in many patients in similar situations and poses a version of Freud's query about the repetition compulsion), I present two explanations relevant to my central theme of the consolidation of symbolic identity. Throughout this work, I emphasized that the ego ideal functions as a support for the lived sense of subjective cohesion or, in more Lacanian terms, as a support for the metonymic chain of discourse enabling participation in the intersubjective exchanges of ordinary life. I see it as a vital link between private experience and communicable affect. In this regard, symbolic identification is impaired by trauma. Wendy's early traumatic experiences were primarily due to the absence of adequate parental holding and presence. We knew from independent sources that her mother was depressed and angry for specific reasons at the time of her birth and had turned to her own career out of conscious resentment at resuming a parental role with her daughter. As an older child, Wendy sought to stimulate herself through eating, immersion in video games, intense daydreams, and, later, masturbation and drug use. Her father's involvement with her sounded intermittent, until she was old enough to accompany him on trips. As an example of mother's loss of interest, Wendy contrasted her older siblings' library of beloved children's books, which her mother had enjoyed reading to them, with her own paltry collection. They had also attended a Sunday school where mother volunteered, which she had been spared. Finally, Wendy told many stories of waiting alone at home with her games or food, only to be criticized harshly upon mother's return. These seem like the conditions cited by Bromberg (1998) as predisposing toward dissociation and lack of integration of parts of self.

Symbolic identification may also have been impaired by father's grandiosity and pseudo self-sufficiency, especially during a period of schism in the marriage, which coincided with his greatest use of Wendy as a substitute love object. To the extent that he may have turned to her as a support for his ideal ego, in effect to serve as his *objet petit a*, she may have been caught between two imaginary subjective positions: as the "nothing sidekick" to father, which he reinforced by including her in *his* specialness, and as the self-indulgent, greedy daughter, where she attempted to fill her inner emptiness and need for love with a culturally designated fantasy ("get high," and "enjoy yourself"). In neither was she a subject of her own desire.

After becoming more aware of her tendency to repeat these positions in her outside relationships, Wendy began to recognize their appearance in the analysis. She noticed that her relationship with me also involved her old desire to please and wondered about her need to persist in this self-defeating pattern. She stopped confessing her inadequacy as a patient (not interesting enough, couldn't possibly understand deep psychoanalytic issues, and the like) and dared to express criticisms of the therapy. She took to heart my interpretation that she kept looking for what I wanted from her and never spoke about what she wanted. In fact, I had made this genre of intervention numerous times without much result. She had rationalized that she needed to learn from me how to use the treatment, which of her many issues were most relevant, whether she was doing well as a patient, and so on. We often seemed to get caught in circular exchanges about her wishing for approval, acceptance, and praise from me by meeting my expectations, which fundamentally reinforced (mirrored) her core imaginary fantasy that I held the key to solving her problems.

A change in the process seemed to occur at a point when I had become annoyed that Wendy had failed to pursue what seemed like important dream material and reverted to her more helpless posture. This irritation was detectable in my comment that she was ignoring the dream content, which may have indicated, paradoxically, that I was not omniscient and did indeed want something of her. She was struck first by my disapproval. "I know you won't be interested in having me as your patient if I don't interpret my dreams," she explained. "Maybe I can't, so it's hopeless." Then, after a pause, she laughed, "This is what I do with all those guys.

'Nothing me,' waiting to be told what to do. Well, maybe I don't know what I want. Maybe I don't want anything, like I'm just a blob." Her hearty laughter continued and then she made a truly insightful comment, "The kids I work with are like that with me."

Indeed, in her work, Wendy was much more clearly identified with her father's style and profession than her mother's. Unconsciously, however, to give up her imaginary relationship with him for a symbolic one would have meant to lose him (by losing the symptomatic fusional link to him as the *objet a*). A fantasy of oneness with her father seemed to stand in the way of being like him in some limited respect while remaining separate. In her associations, Wendy presented different representations of this loss. At a conscious level, she wouldn't need him anymore, and he would have no use for her in a new, independent role. This realization involved grieving. There was also the threat of arousing the anger of her mother and siblings (if she stopped being the problem child and thereby exposed the serious difficulties of the others). These fears began to emerge more explicitly, as well as a newly voiced homosexual concern, as she feared her caring for women might become sexualized. These latter anxieties also suggested earlier developmental deficits in the relationship with mother, which her identification with father may have served in part to patch over. In a similar way, Kohut might have seen the idealization of her father as an attempt to compensate for failures in early mirroring.

The exploration of our transferential relationship enabled us to understand the resistances to change and the powerful attachment to the fantasy pleasures of the side-kick role. Her idealization of me as the all-knowing analyst was a piece of this dynamic, and we could both see ways in which I had been complicit in enjoying the admiring submission she had described with other men. Eventually, Wendy desired to be treated that way herself by a loving man. Of course, in summarizing in this manner, I am highlighting only one strand of an analytic process in which the concepts of desire and of the *objet petit a* seemed to have brought clarification and order. Others would certainly find other useful perspectives to illuminate a complex analytic experience. With this caveat in mind, I leap to the end of Wendy's analysis. This phase revolved essentially around her new object choice of a man as different as one could be from her father. In the Lacanian model, every subject is equally different from every other differentiated subject within the symbolic order. However, it may have not been happenstance that

Wendy's lover had a significant physical deficit and could only but admire her physical prowess. Something felt right to her about this relationship, which seemed such a departure from the past, and she experienced a new desire to have a child by this man. One could hypothesize that the basis of her new love was, as Lacan insisted, perception of the lack in the other. This deficiency or vulnerability evokes the fantasy of the *objet petit a* (as the missing part, which, we recall, functions as cause of desire).

We might surmise that analysis helped Wendy to create and affirm her difference, rather than reenact another version of the same fantasy relation with her father. As we saw in chapter 2, the dual relationship in fantasy corresponds to Lacan's conception of the mirror transference. It is an attempt to avoid fragmentation by identification with an image. One way of understanding the change in Wendy from a Lacanian perspective is in terms of a shift away from this totalistic imaginary identification as one to a symbolic internalization as another (by a partial identification with a set of traits). This step leads to a different structural relationship with the *objet petit a,* which becomes external to the self and, thereby, falls away (the acceptance of incompleteness in the self and other placing the *objet petit a* outside, that is, a fantasy to be pursued along the normal paths of desire). By intervening at the level of her identification with her father rather than focusing on her unhappiness and acting out, or on her unmet needs for mothering, for example, I supported Wendy's symbolic identity against an imaginary one. She could then relinquish the fusional fantasy and own her own separate wishes and desires.

In the transference, I moved from reincarnating an imaginary mirror relationship with the father as an ideal self toward a position of sustaining the lack in the Other (by wanting, by not knowing, by being unable to gratify her). Our small contretemps about her passive stance toward associating in the session (and others like it, of course) restaged this configuration and brought home to us what was a stake in the side-kick bond. We had not developed a real relationship on a personal or social level, although something intense had transpired between us. A piece of the past had been restaged—a piece that had been presaged by her initial dream. By the end of the analysis there were significant shifts in her position (and, to some extent, my own), which enabled Wendy to let go of the jouissance of a repetition and freed her to be the subject of her own desire.

6

— · —

The Man Who Didn't Exist: The Case of Louis Althusser

— · —

*It was necessary that I plunge myself into the void
to reach at last the solution of that* beginning from
nothing *which had become the form of my problem.*
—LOUIS ALTHUSSER, *Lettres à Franca*

LOUIS ALTHUSSER (1918–1990) WAS A PROMINENT MARXIST PHILOSO-
pher and student of psychoanalytic theory whose writings had a
major impact on the Left in France and other countries. As the
epitome of the committed intellectual endeavoring to address the
inequities of the world, his teaching and actions inspired his students at the elite *École Normale Superieure* and at the Sorbonne
for over 20 years. His scholarly books and articles had a private
counterpart in a contrapuntal personal reflection in letters and conversations about his own fragile subjectivity. The chapter opening
quotation from a letter to his lover Franca Madonia (Althusser,
1998), which summarized his awareness of the motive for his passionate involvement with the works of Machiavelli, is a good example. The Prince as a subject, emerging in a chance concatenation
of events as from nothing to found a new state, was an alter ego
for Althusser, who struggled with his own unformed "state." From
a young age, he was tortured by a painful sense of unreality, eventually seeking help in two lengthy therapies after a series of mental
breakdowns that would today be diagnosed as Bipolar Disorder.

The nadir of this disturbance was reached on the morning of November 16, 1980, with the bizarre strangulation of his wife, Hélène Rytmann, a crime for which he was never tried because of mental illness. Five years afterward, in *L'Avenir Dure Longtemps*, an autobiography baring his soul to the public, Althusser sought to explain and justify himself by retracing the path that had led him to this tragic point.[1] The project seems in many respects equivalent to that of Senatspräsident Schreber, mined by Freud for his theory of psychosis. It offers a demonstration of what is at once most familiar to clinicians (the repetitive phenomenology of a major mental disorder) and unfathomable (the unique individual case), and presents the strange dichotomy in Althusser's writings between his psychoanalytic reading of his individual fate as a subject determined by a history and the more radical and nihilistic philosophy of pure chance and self-creation that he found in Machiavelli.

Althusser (1985a) wrote poignantly of attempting to appear to be what he could not be, lacking "an authentic existence of my own" (p. 107). He felt disembodied and unreal, attributing his deficiency to an originary maternal gaze that looked through him toward another person, his deceased namesake. "Death was inscribed from the beginning in me," he wrote. "I wanted to destroy myself at any price because, since always, I did not exist" (p. 306). In the view of some commentators (see de Pommier, 1998; de Marty, 1999), Althusser's fascination with a philosophy of the void, of nothingness, flowed from this self-perception. After rejecting his early Catholic, then Marxist humanism, he developed a brutal form of materialism, finally pronouncing the structuralist verdict of "the death of man" and proposing in his last papers a philosophy of history without subjects, a theory of origins from "the nothingness of cause, of essence, and of origin" (Althusser, 1985b, p. 492). In this ultimate conception, there was no place for agency, a cohesive project of selfhood, or intentionality. The materialist philosopher, he declared, was one who boards a moving train by accident, "not knowing where it is going or where he is headed" (p. 480). Of course, there can be no "explaining away" the insights of a brilliant philosopher like Althusser, whose ideas have obviously been

---

[1]The complex history of this document published posthumously is recounted in the Preface to *L'Avenir Dure Longtemps*, by Olivier Corpet and Yann Boutang (1992).

shared by many unafflicted thinkers and that often strike one as a profound knowledge. Freud (1917) wrote of the melancholic that he possesses a keener eye for the truth than others, very near to self-knowledge, but wondered why a man must become ill to discover this truth. The autobiography does, however, leave one with the disturbing sense of a bad-faith program of self-justification.

BIOGRAPHY[2]

Louis Althusser was born in 1918 in a small Algerian town, the son of an Alsacian banker, Charles Althusser, and a French mother, Lucienne Berger. He had one younger sister, Georgette, who also suffered severe depressions. The family saga was emphasized, to put it mildly, in his two autobiographical works (there was an earlier effort, *Les Faits,* 1976a) in which he insisted upon his place in his mother's unconscious as the replacement for a lost love, that for his deceased uncle Louis, for whom he was named. The original Louis Althusser was preparing to enter an elite academy when he was drafted and eventually killed in battle, leaving a bereft fiancée, Lucienne. Into his vacated place stepped an older brother, Charles, who became the replacement groom and, nine months later, the father of another Louis. By this sole act, Althusser concluded, his destiny was already determined by the place he came to occupy as signifier of his dead namesake, the desire of his mother and his father's rival. Lacan might have said that the dice were already thrown for him before his birth, and, without any doubt, Althusser's familiarity with Lacanian concepts, along with his own experiences as a patient, contributed substantially to his conclusions.

Reading Althusser's autobiography, one would have to be convinced that he was a pathetic wreck of a nonperson, stunted in emotional development from earliest childhood and never existing as a true subject. The harshness of his relentless self-reproaches does resemble Freud's portrait of the melancholic, but there was always an element of contrivance and ruse in Althusser, who in

---

[2]For the material in this section I am indebted to the magisterial biographic study by Yann Moulier Boutang (1992) and to notes by O. Corpet, Y. M. Boutang, and François Matheron in the autobiography (Corpet and Boutang, 1992), collected philosophical and political writings (Corpet and Matheron, 1996), and writings on psychoanalysis (Matheron, 1995).

part played the part of a psychiatric victim. Nonetheless, there is no dispute that Althusser had terrible psychiatric and emotional problems. Apart from his documented episodes of mental illness, beginning at Sainte Anne Hospital in 1947, Althusser was from childhood an inhibited and insecure man, extremely vulnerable to criticism, failure, or success, as well to physical ailments, any of which might provoke extreme anxiety, withdrawal, or depression. Another indication of his frailty was a stunted sexual development, which he blamed on two subjectively emasculating interventions by his mother during his adolescence. She is said to have objected to his visiting a female acquaintance and to have uttered comments about the stain of a nocturnal emission. Be that as it may, he did display a near-phobic avoidance of women as a young man, and claimed not to have masturbated until age 27. Hélène Rytman, his eventual wife, was, in fact, his first sexual partner, and their liaison triggered the depression that culminated in his initial hospitalization.

All the same, the youthful Althusser showed many strengths and excelled in many areas. From the first, he was a brilliant student, drew well, enjoyed athletic pursuits, was a talented violinist, and, in general, was more engaged in the real world than he would have his readers believe. Perhaps more important, he had the ability to form close friendships. His biography does show that he suffered from the lack of a warm relationship with a stiff, old-fashioned sort of father, a situation worsened by the extreme emotional schism between the parents. For her part, his mother was obsessed with health and religion in an eccentric manner long before the onset of her own serious depressive illness. On the other hand, his biographer, Boutang, cites signs of warmth and concern between father and son, and Althusser's letters from captivity evidenced a conventional family devotion, which raises questions about his claim that Charles never loved his offspring and thereby refused the symbolic paternal function.

As a youth, Althusser was deeply involved in Catholic religious observance. In this he echoed the piety of his familial and social milieu. At Lyon, as a lycée student, he participated actively in religious retreats and moved in conservative Catholic and monarchist circles, but, after the war, he was attracted to the progressive Catholic workers' movement. Eventually, he broke with the Church and its left wing of humanist politics, although it is not clear when his religious faith was finally abandoned or lost. The reasons for his progression toward the Left were probably not very different from those of many French Catholics in the wake of fascism and the cold war, disatisfied with the status quo and seeking a more just society. No doubt Althusser's intense religious belief sustained him for many years, gradually to be replaced in fervor by a commitment to the new ideology and politics of the French Communist Party (PCF).

One document bearing on his evolution away from religious humanism is a posthumously published paper entitled, "On Conjugal Obscenity" (Sur l'Obscenité Conjugale; Althusser, 1951). In this work, from what might in later years have been described as a radical feminist perspective, he attacked the Church's efforts to promote a spiritual partnership between husband and wife on the basis of a shared religious vision. With respect to his argument, two comments might be in order. First, Althusser could not seem to conceive that a couple might find fulfillment in shared devotion to religious ideals in spite of, or even because of, necessary secular renunciations. He recognized the potential sacrifice on the part of the married woman of opportunities for intellectual or creative growth but apparently not the importance of balancing productive achievement with emotional satisfaction (for both partners). Second, this lack of balance goes to the heart of his long and stormy relationship with his partner, Hélène. Certainly, their shared commitment to communism, an ideal which Hélène pursued with passion, was the basis of a relationship that did not seek children nor the customary accoutrements of bourgeois married life. Yet, throughout their lives together, Althusser needed to turn to other women for emotional and sexual satisfaction, perhaps unable to come to terms with his dependency upon a single woman. Later, in an unpublished piece, he attacked feminism (as a movement), making it clear that he regarded women as holding power over men.

In the autobiography, he spoke of his mother as brutalized by an insensitive, domineering father, and one can infer from these comments an identification with her, which Althusser certainly resisted. As I will elaborate, the failure of a symbolic paternal identification left Althusser in an imaginary dual relation with a mother who could seem by turns weak and defective or all-powerful, hence a series of unsuccessful attempts to triangulate or to create a symbolic third to provide a space for separation and subjectivization. His portrayal of his mother (although he noted the difference between his internal parents and the real ones) was rather monstrous, and suggests the threat of fusion and the narcissistic hatred analyzed by Lacan as part of the mirror relationship. This dynamic seems intrinsic to Althusser's subsequent relationships with other women as well. Possibly, what Boutang (1997) suggested as a suppressed incestuous dynamic with his sister, Georgette, also played a role in these repetitions.

Althusser's fledgling academic career was interrupted by war. He was inducted with his fellow lycéens and assigned to an artillery unit until the French surrender and his removal to a prisoner of war work camp in Germany, where he was to remain almost five years. From this point, his failure to attempt the escape that was on every prisoner's mind occupied an important place in his autobiography and self-analysis. When he did make an effort to falsify his records to pass as a nurse, entitling him to return to occupied France, he commited a careless mistake, which sabotaged his plan. He attributed his behavior to a fear of danger and a need for protection, which kept him from leaving the stalag. There was always a kind of security to be found "on the inside" for a fragile spirit like Althusser who, moreover, was able to make strong friendships and do useful work within the confines of the all-male camp. Other authors have commented at length on his analogous relationship to other institutions, beginning with the Church and extending to the École Normale Supérieure, where he was to reside for most of his adult life, and, most dramatically, with the French Communist Party.

A critical insider, who took his distance from the institutions within which he functioned, Althusser seemed to require the paradoxical status of adherence and transcendance, a kind of "having it both ways." Although no one could have been a more dedicated professor, he mocked the pretensions of philosophy as "blah-blah." A lifelong member of the PCF, he came to contest most of its major ideological positions. Something analogous occurred in his important male relationships in which he insisted that he could never accept a master, a standoff repeated in the case of his own analyst, René Diatkine, which he called his impossible ambition to be "father to the father." With women, a passionate approach followed by flight or equivocation seems to have been characteristic, a graphic example of which was his touching and exasperating correspondence with Franca Madonia. She appeared in his early letters as the answer to everything, yet he could not commit to making a life with her. As in another intense love affair with Claire, he could not give up Hélène, whom he tried to incorporate impossibly into each new relationship. Sometimes his behavior in exposing Hélène to these women was quite callous, which he acknowledged; yet, although he could treat her quite abusively, he also needed her as a protective object, someone who buffered all other important commitments.

There was a peculiar dynamic at work in Althusser that extended beyond a simple conflict of ambivalence. One could speculate that in his quest to shore up an enfeebled self, Althusser required relationships with powerful others, but these must have also posed a serious threat. Like the severely narcissistic patients described by Modell (1984), who find a point of psychic equilibrium in the position he called "the sphere within a sphere" (p. 34), Althusser may have maintained a kind of imaginary self-cohesion by remaining within the protective envelope of a person or institution toward which he could profess independence. The sphere is a compromise between total isolation and dangerous confrontation with an object who might invalidate and negate one's existence. Thus he could not sustain closeness with the friends and teachers who might have served as mentors, nor with the women who loved him, all sacrificed to a grandiose fantasy of self-creation and self-sufficiency. In restaging this pattern, Althusser may have attempted to locate a "third" of separation to free him from imaginary identification with his mother, but, in every case, the person or institution he chose became assimilated into the old mirroring structure that had to be resisted—hence his tenuous solution to become the "outsider–insider," or "father to the father," simultaneously remaining within (contained in the dual relation) and beyond.

Following repatriation, Althusser began graduate studies in philosophy at the École Normale Supérieure (ENS), where he spent the next 34 years. Upon acceptance of his thesis on Hegel in 1949, he was offered a faculty position. In 1948, he had joined the Communist Party. In the eyes of many, his progressive move leftward owed everything to the influence of Hélène Rytmann, whom he had met toward the end of 1946. They developed an instant complicity, based in large part on their shared identification with the working class and a commitment to revolutionary change, but it seems highly probable that Althusser was heading irresistibly toward communism with or without her. A certain logical rigor led him to accept the party as the sole viable vehicle for the revolutionary transformation of European civilization. At a deeper level, the void at the heart of an increasingly formal religious commitment may have compelled a replacement as a bulwark against the madness by which he sensed himself threatened.[3] More than most, Althusser needed to adhere body and soul to a representation of an ideal. His lycée thesis, consecrated to the God of Faith (Boutang, 1992), may have been the high-water mark of this devotion. Boutang concludes that Althusser dropped the sanctified language of his youth after a depression in 1943 in the stalag. In his despair, Althusser may have lost his vital link to God, suddenly facing the unbridgeable Augustinian gap.

What might have been the consequences of this loss? Here, we can share de Pommier's (1998) Lacanian hypothesis that God for Althusser functioned as "a third term," a god of separation, occupying a role for which his father had been already forever disqualified. For Lacan, when the paternal function is assumed by the actual father and supported by the mother, the internalization of a symbolic law institutes an ego ideal, freeing the child from the impasse of the mirror stage of dyadic relations. The ego ideal represents an inscription of a sign and, later, signifiers of the father, which install an identification (Lacan, 1960–1961). As I interpret this process, what becomes internalized on the basis of an inaugural identificatory trace is a set of narratives or, perhaps, multimodal representations, which permit translation between intrapsychic experience and intersubjective speech. Symbolic representations of affect in the form of model situations and narratives are crucial in channeling private emotions into sharable discourse that others can understand and respond to. The third term of Lacan itself refers to a mediating function between subject and unfamiliar others, creating what Winnicott might have named a transitional space, imbued simultaneously with personal and public meanings. From this perspective, the various people or institutions that Althusser

---

[3]The importance of the term *void* (*vide*) for Althusser cannot be underestimated, playing both a negative and positive role. His efforts to work out a non-Hegelian function for negativity as the site of the *surgissement* (eruption) of self-creation and the paradoxical relationship of this void to Lacan's concepts of full and empty speech are discussed by Matheron (1997).

sought as replacements for this deficient function were bound to fall short.

The circumstances of the murder were as follows. In the course of a highly productive period, Althusser developed symptoms of a hiatal hernia. After a routine surgical procedure, he awoke with restless anxiety that soon progressed into a severe depression. His alarmed physicians told him that he was now displaying classic symptoms of melancholia for the first time. He was rehospitalized and various medications were tried, one of which may have induced a toxic delirium. He recounted symptoms of profound regression, confusion, and paranoia. Upon discharge home in the company of Hélène, he was not fully recovered, and their relationship seemed to disintegrate into a destructive configuration of shared despair and self-hatred from which she tried, according to his autobiography, to extricate herself, only to arouse the keenest separation anxiety on the part of her husband. Diatkine, who had by then reluctantly become Hélène's psychotherapist, urged rehospitalization. From this point, the facts are unknown, Althusser claiming amnesia for the crucial events. There was no evidence of a struggle. The philosopher came to his senses while feeling fatigue in his arms as he gently massaged the inert neck of his wife, as he had often done at her request. The picture he painted in his account was one of her complicity in the strangulation, as though she had wished a release from their shared inferno—*un suicide par personne interposée*.[4]

The strangeness of the scenario recounted by Althusser was all the more eerie for seeming to have been lifted in almost unmodified form from a dream he had transcribed 16 years earlier. The dream followed closely upon the receipt of a letter from Hélène, insensitively diagnosing his family's pathology. Obviously stung, he had written back to her that the letter "touched him to the quick" that, like the lightning, "it illuminates and it kills" (Althusser, 1964, p. 428). In his dream, Althusser had to murder a complicit

---

[4]The phrase *suicide par personne interposée* (suicide by an intermediary), recalls Althusser's "Three Notes on the Theory of Discourse," (1966) in which he defined four modes of subjectivity (or "effects-of-subject") in the third of which, aesthetic discourse, subjectivity was present via *personnes interposées* (see Žižek, 1994, for a discussion of this problematic of Althusserian subjectivity). This association with an aesthetic concept makes the murder a theatrical gesture in which Althusser did not participate as a subject of his own unconscious or desire.

sister in "a sort of pathetic communion by sacrifice" (p. 429). The recorded dream was discovered by a friend four years after the actual murder. Even earlier, in 1961, in a letter to Franca (Althusser, 1998), he had written that Hélène called for help while refusing help, "almost like a battered child" (p. 72), and that she defended herself against the person coming to her aid as though he were going to strangle her!

INTELLECTUAL CONTRIBUTIONS

Commentators have attempted to link Althusser's crime and psychopathology to his theoretical positions, notably the evolution of an antisubjectivist philosophy from what originally had been a set of humanist ideals. We can trace this passage in his passionate rereading of Marx and, especially, the structural theory that organized his interpretation. Who speaks of Marx must inevitably talk about Hegel and the tradition of German idealist philosophy in which Althusser was expert, and, in many respects, he could be said to have been engaged in a lifelong struggle with the legacy of the great philosopher. Like so many of his important relationships, Althusser's encounter with Hegel was one of ambivalence, as if the exalted idealism of the Phenomenology and its belief in the inexorability of the historical dialectic exercised both a powerful appeal and a repugnance, just as the Christian faith of his youth and the communism of his maturity. In his master's thesis, Althusser (1947) developed an original argument in which Hegel's awareness of the material existence of mankind in specific historical forms had replaced a metaphysical conception of history. For the youthful Althusser, this philosophical materialism provided a framework from which a Marxist humanist concern for the oppressed could derive its justification.

> The entire revolutionary effort, [he wrote] could be considered as the taking possession of the transcendant by the empiric, of the form by the contents. This is why the Marxist movement is a materialism . . . but also a humanism. . . . Revolutionary action can conceive, at least formally, of the coming to be of the human totality reconciled with its own structure [p. 222].

This exalted attempt to harmonize Marxist praxis with Hegelian humanism was to come to an abrupt close.

In a manner reminiscent of his loss of religious faith, Althusser rejected the Marxist appropriation of Hegel's myth of the dialectic of history, concluding that Marxist dialectics was simply bad philosophy. Even earlier, however, he had become hostile to the common notion that Marx had built upon inherited Hegelianism (via the philosophy of Feuerbach), a seemingly inescapable proposition that Althusser was at pains to refute. Instead, he argued that Marx broke decisively with both thinkers, totally abandoning a humanistic focus on the individual subject as the agent of history. In what is by now a familiar structuralist move, he insisted that history in the form of structures of economic relationships and modes of production created the forms of human subjectivity. The conscious subject was an effect and not the center or cause of historical process. In this formulation, the concept of an independent, individual subject was seen as a historical construction belonging to a particular time and social class. Althusser (1968) asserted that Marx represented "a prodigious tearing away from his origins" (p. 80), turning from individuals toward societies as the true subjects of history. This "displacement," he wrote in a notorious phrase, dispensed with "the theoretical services of a concept of man" (p. 256). Here as elsewhere, Althusser's single-minded focus on structural forces ignored their dynamic relationship with the individual subject, who thereby became an epiphenomenon.[5] Could this theory have been a reflection of a personal struggle to grasp his own life objectively—that is, as a psychiatric patient determined by a "condition"—and subjectively—as a unique psychological subject? This question touches upon the roots of his early interest in psychoanalysis.

Unusual for his time, Althusser began reading a variety of psychoanalytic texts as a student, citing Freud in his own thesis. Lacan came to his attention in the 1950s, when Althusser began to read his publications in a new review, *La psychanalyse*. In 1963, he

---

[5]See, for example, Althusser's *Réponse à John Lewis* (1973), in which he deemed the category of "man" illusory and fetishistic. Lewis (1972), a British Marxist, had stated that "the best cure for a toothache is not to cut off the patient's head" (p. 24).

mentioned Lacan's work positively in an article, which brought
him to the attention of the master, then in the throes of his traumatic
inquisition by the International Psychoanalytic Association.
Althusser lectured and organized a seminar on psychoanalysis at
the ENS, publishing his well-known text, "Freud et Lacan" in the
Marxist review *Nouvelle Critique,* at the end of 1964. That same
year, he invited the excommunicated Lacan to bring his seminar to
the ENS. Although Althusser reported only once attending Lacan's
seminar, he was familiar with the *Écrits,* an annotated copy of which
was found in his library. His articles credited Lacan with grasping
the essential in Freud, and here he broached what would be developed with utter consistency in his subsequent writings, namely the
role of theory in advancing scientific knowledge. In what could be
viewed as either a measure of his genius or a kind of excessive
intellectualism, Althusser insisted on the profound importance for
psychoanalysis of moving beyond the status of a mere collection of
interesting observations, empirical findings, and practical manipu-
lations of technique toward a comprehensive theory.

In "Freud and Lacan," written for a mainly hostile, leftist au-
dience, Althusser (1964) performed a combined ideological critique
of the institutional functions of psychoanalysis, especially its revisionist American versions, which he condemned, and an "episte-
mological elucidation" of its original concepts, which he defended.
These concepts had to do above all with a new object, the unconscious, of what he termed a new science, psychoanalysis, unlike
the other human sciences. Against the revisionist vision of a normal
ego shaped by evolution to fit an expectable reality, Althusser situated the coming to be of the human subject as an uncertain journey,
an "eruption," which emerged from and split the natural order. At
this time, he closely followed Lacan's reading of Freud, notably
around the structuring function of language in producing a divided
subject. With this development, he saw the possibility for a *science*
of psychoanalysis, provided that the lingering traces of *ideology*
and of *ritual* could be separated from true theoretical understanding.

More than 10 years later, Althusser again took up this issue in
two papers to be submitted to a groundbreaking symposium in the
USSR on the theme of "the unconscious." Here he articulated a
problem that in some ways remains at the heart of the current
state of psychoanalysis. That is, is psychoanalysis a simple practice
"occasionally yielding results," to be understood, at best, as a vari-

ant of neurobiology, developmental psychology, and related fields or, at worst, as mere technique without a theory? Although Althusser recognized the necessity of integration with other disciplines, he upheld the importance of a unique science of the unconscious. In this respect, Althusser (1976b) first praised Lacan's contribution as an *attempt* at mediation between an outmoded biophysical theory of psychoanalysis and current scientific and philosophical models. The tone then shifted to one of stringent criticism of the results of Lacan's project, which he described as "teetering on the pedestal of its uncertain theses" (p. 92). He wrote that instead of a scientific theory of the unconscious, Lacan had given us a "fantastic" philosophy of psychoanalysis, which basically "duped everybody." Althusser withdrew his first paper in reaction to fierce criticisms by his associates, notably Elisabeth Roudinesco (see Althusser, 1976c), and Lacan disappeared from Althusser's second submission, "On Marx and Freud" (1976d).

Although Althusser's conception of psychoanalysis owed a great deal to Lacan, he also understood how drives (in the Freudian sense, 1985a, pp. 121–122) and early mothering (in the Winnicottian sense [p. 238]) work toward creating an embodied subject. Eventually, he became disillusioned with Lacan, and this must have had important consequences for him. Did his high-intensity intellect burn its way through Lacanism, or was the personal factor crucial? Clearly, Lacan never reciprocated the enthusiasm and warmth conveyed in Althusser's letters to him, while profiting from his influence to conduct his seminar at the ENS.

Some of Althusser's sentiments were expressed in his account of the suicide of his student, Lucien Sebag, who was an analysand of Lacan. Lacan's demeanor when he came to inform him of the event appalled Althusser. He confided that he had been obliged to drop Sebag as a patient "for technical reasons" (Althusser, 1985a), because Sebag had fallen in love with Lacan's daughter, Judith. Althusser wrote that he restrained himself from asking Lacan why he had not hospitalized his suicidal patient. He commented,

> I have very often wondered what he would have done in my own case if I had been one of his patients. . . . Would he have left me without protection so as not to infringe the slightest analytic rule . . . rules which in the mind of Freud were never imperatives? . . . Let me be forgiven for having reported this,

but through the unhappy Sebag, whom I loved a lot, and Judith,
whom I knew fairly well, the story also concerned me [Althusser,
1985a, p. 213].

Here, Althusser spelled out his need for protection of his own vulnerable self. Disillusionment with a former hero must have been
damaging for him, just as coming too close might have been. Instead,
he maintained his familiar "insider–outsider" position in relation
to Lacanian psychoanalysis, choosing for himself a Freudian analyst who had left Lacan. In the end, he was thrown back from his
religious teachers and the Church, the PCF, and Lacan onto Hélène
as his most reliable, if deeply flawed, protective sphere.

There was a final disillusioning experience with Lacan more
than 15 years after Sebag's suicide. Lacan had decided for his own
obscure reasons to dissolve his analytic training program, the École
Freudienne, summoning his followers to a gathering at a Paris hotel. Althusser's puzzling behavior at this meeting, which had abso-
lutely nothing to do with him personally or professionally, bears
study. After all, what was it to him that this latest incarnation of a
Lacan-dominated institution was about to go the way of its prede-
cessors? No doubt that it would soon be reborn in other forms.
Yet Althusser was beside himself, as he gained uninvited access to
the stormy assembly of analysts. Althusser's (1980) argument was
against the foolishness and political manipulation of Lacan's followers and for the welfare of the proletariat of patients, whose
fates he felt were in some sense at stake in this debacle. In what
sense? Analysts and patients would continue to work together in
offices and clinics regardless of the institutional politics of the profession, which change all the time. Yet Althusser knew better than
most that individuals draw their sustenance from social systems,
and that when an institution is discredited, the work itself eventually suffers. Human social arrangements are fragile, so that, for
Althusser, a great deal was at stake, not the least important of
which was his own well-being as an analysand. At the meeting of
the École, the symbolic containing sphere of psychoanalysis was
shattering before his eyes. If Lacanian politics had turned rotten
and Freudianism was held hostage by the revisionist Americans,
what hope remained for him to be cured?

The core psychoanalytic problem addressed by Althusser, that
of the proper conceptualization of the human subject, rests on a

paradox. One can hold that individuals are responsible for what they become, perhaps in terms of their earliest psychic choices, yet at the same time are caught in unconscious patterns laid down outside their subjective awareness. It is a paradox implicit in clinical psychoanalysis, which aims at enlarging the scope of freedom through a reconstructive reliving of early experience and the subjective assumption of a path already taken. This is the ambiguity criticized with some success by Sartre in his discussion of bad faith, where he performed a kind of *reductio ad absurdum* on the Freudian unconscious. In its place, he proposed his concept of the *poursoi* (for itself), the self as pure project, which takes responsibility for itself in the inevitability of choice. Althusser, like the other structuralists, was profoundly antipathetic to Sartre's idealization of the individual agent, which he called "a happy psychosis." For Sartre (1943), freedom was the basic human condition to be accepted. "Man being condemned to be free carries the weight of the whole world on his shoulders: he is responsible for the world and for himself as a way of being" (pp. 553–554). For Althusser, this position repeated the fallacy of conceiving of the individual subject as a unity and as the point of departure for knowledge. Although he recognized that psychoanalysis is a theory of the individual mind (the unconscious belongs to the individual) and that ideologies involve unconscious fantasies, he refused to accept the subjectivity Lacan based upon the signifier—on the human transformation from natural creature to symbolic subject in the realm of language. At this point, it might be said that Althusser's self-analysis came apart on the shoals of his refusal to accept that history is made by man, however blindly or carelessly (see the criticism by John Lewis, 1972, and his response; Althusser, 1973). What Althusser presented as his personal tragedy of the absence of an embodied self was undermined by the antihumanism of his former Stalinist politics and his final conception of a history without subjects.

Contrary to Althusser, we could admit that psychoanalysis, perhaps like Marxism, sits ambiguously between humanism and science, and there are many indications that it has begun to assume that paradox, even as it struggles uneasily with its problem of self-definition. Of course, Althusser, Sartre, and Lacan were correct. There is no *en-soi* (in-itself) in the unconscious. That interpretation of Freudian determinism is untenable. Even though we have a sense of character as destiny unfolding outside our command, there is no script for it. Likewise, there is no entity we could isolate as "the subject" or "the self," yet we seem bound to fall back on some such construct, even on the notion of an experiencing subject, anathema as it is to structuralist thought. As Althusser (1955) wrote in relation to a disagreement between Paul Ricoeur and Raymond Aron, this is a debate about how a philosophy of realism can be applied to history or, analogously, to psychoanalysis. That is, concepts and ideas, like Freudian constructs about "the mental apparatus," must refer to something in the real. For the scientific realist, there must be a truth beyond the idea. Althusser was fond of quoting Spinoza's epigram, "the concept of the dog that does not bark." For Lacan, the beyond of conscious experience was not in the physical body but in the materiality of language, in the signifier, which carried the desiring subject helplessly in its wake.[6] Althusser rejected this model of a subject pursuing her unique desire, locating the source of human actions in the accidental *conjoncture* of events, which unpredictably gels or "takes" as a transient shape without significance or cause.

THE MAN WHO DIDN'T EXIST

How can we understand Althusser's refusal of subjective responsibility? Certainly he was an sick man, with a severe form of bipolar illness, yet most persons with this diagnosis do not suffer from his painful sense of a lack of existence, nor become murderers, nor develop a bleak philosophy like his version of materialism (however valid in some sense it may be). So psychiatry in the end does not take us very far in understanding his case. If, the sense of a genuine existence derives from the suturing of the embodied, desiring subject to a set of ideals, to a symbolic framework beyond the self that gives coherence and meaning, Althusser's difficulties may be traceable in part to his failure to sustain this connection. Many details of his history suggest Althusser's exquisite narcissistic vulnerability and would seem to support the formulation made earlier of his "sphere within a sphere" position as a specific solution to a

---

[6]This formulation is not quite right in the context of Lacan's later writings, which treat the concept of the real, including the real of the body, more systematically. Language or the symbolic depend ultimately upon this real, albeit in an indirect manner.

precarious psychic condition. We could also speak of his difficulty sustaining a cohesive self or of supporting his existence as a speaking subject in the face of his own unmediated desires and the desires of others. Althusser sought out intense relationships and permitted himself to acknowledge great emotional dependency on them (and not in an exclusively manipulative way), but he needed to maintain a safe distance. Indeed, it seems most characteristic of him to have pursued such bonds from his earliest youth. I believe that Althusser's early self-diagnosis was correct. He required his religious faith to survive, and he needed living people to represent that faith. He found many such, and yet the faith did not hold. As we have seen, he moved from a pious Catholicism toward a humanistic Marxist–Christian militancy and, finally, to communism of the *pure et dure* variety. Along the way, psychoanalysis, via the charismatic figure of Jacques Lacan, came to play for him an important role.

Probably, none of these institutions were able to bear the weight Althusser needed to place on them. He formulated idealistic visions of Christianity, communism, and psychoanalysis that went beyond, or even at times flatly contradicted the ideologies of those institutions, and he became in the process a kind of subversive adherent, working to transform them into something they could not become. Althusser was one of those comparatively rare individuals who, in their discomfort with what exists, want to change the world. This aspiration is usually associated with intellectual brilliance, a touch of grandiosity, and a coming-of-age at a particular historic moment, all of which describe him. Beyond these generic explanatory factors, we must turn to the underlying "contents" of his thought—the problem of finding viable ideals, their internalization in the form of an ego ideal, and their role in sustaining a connection to a broader cultural framework that can support the individual subject. In Lacanian terms, we might speak of the human necessity of locating a singular place within the symbolic order.

Lacking the symbolic identification that might have installed an ego ideal, Althusser needed to rely upon an imaginary other who could support cohesion by mirroring, provided that this other could be kept at a manageable distance. At the same time, I have argued, he unsuccessfully sought a true "third" for symbolic identification, foreclosed by his particular family history (the disqualification of his father). Failing to achieve this, he was left in the pseudo self-sufficient position of the inner sphere, a grandiose imaginary self, requiring a containing other person or institution whose importance he could deny. Modell's (1984) description suggests that a powerful affective charge—too strong feelings for the object— can burst the inner bubble. The subject's fractured shell is then unable to resist the overwhelming intrusion of needs and emotions into the virtual space that buffers the contained from the containing objects. Hélène may have performed this container function for Althusser through her incarnation of the Communist ideal, all the purer for being outside of the Party herself. Their relationship could be characterized as consisting of an oscillation between an insupportable distance and an unbearable and destructive closeness. In strangling her, he may have been attacking that personified container, which could no longer contain or protect him from his empty melancholy.

References

Allouch, J. (1984), *Allô, Lacan? Certainement Pas* [*Hello, Lacan? Certainly Not*]. Paris: EPEL.

Althusser, L. (1947), Du contenu dans la pensée de G. W. F. Hegel [On the contained in the thought of G. W. F. Hegel]. In: *Écrits Philosophiques et Politiques, Tome 1.* Paris: Stock/IMEC, 1994, pp. 59–246.

———— (1951), Sur l'obscenité conjugale [On conjugal obscenity]. In: *Écrits Philosophiques et Politiques, Tome 1.* Paris: Stock/IMEC, 1994, pp. 335–350.

———— (1955), Sur l'objectivité de l'histoire, lettre à Paul Ricoeur [On the objectivity of history, letter to Paul Ricoeur]. *Revue de l'Enseignement Philosophique,* 4:6–13.

———— (1963), La philosophie et les sciences humaines [Philosophy and the human sciences]. *Revue de l'Enseignement Philosophique,* 5:15–16.

———— (1964), Freud and Lacan. In: *Writings on Psychoanalysis,* ed. O. Corpet & F. Matheron (trans. J. Mehlman). New York: Columbia University Press, 1996, pp. 7–32.

———— (1966), Trois notes sur la théories des discours. In: *Écrits sur la Psychanalyse.* Paris: IMEC/Stock, 1993.

———— (1968), *Pour Marx* [*For Marx*]. Paris: Maspero.

———— (1973), *Réponse à John Lewis* [*Response to John Lewis*]. Paris: Maspero.

———— (1976a), Les faits [The facts]. In: *L'Avenir Dure Longtemps* [*The Future Lasts Forever: A Memoir*], ed. O. Corpet & Y. M. Bougang (trans. R. Veasey). Paris: Éditions Stock/IMEC, 1992, pp. 319–400.

———— (1976b), The discovery of Dr. Freud. In: *Writings on Psychoanalysis,* ed. O. Corpet & F. Matheron (trans. J. Mehlman). New York: Columbia University Press, 1996, pp. 85–105.

———— (1976c), Appendix: Letter to Elizabeth Roudinesco. In: *Writings on Psychoanalysis*, ed. O. Corpet & F. Matheron (trans. J. Mehlman). New York: Columbia University Press, 1996, pp. 104–105.

———— (1976d), On Marx and Freud. In: *Writings on Psychoanalysis*, ed. O. Corpet & F. Matheron (trans. J. Mehlman). New York: Columbia University Press, 1996, pp. 105–124.

———— (1980), Complementary remarks on the meeting of March 15, 1980 at the Hotel PLM St. Jacques. In: *Writings on Psychoanalysis*, ed. O. Corpet & F. Matheron (trans. J. Mehlman). New York: Columbia University Press, 1996, pp. 135–143.

———— (1985), *L'Avenir Dure Longtemps* [*The Future Lasts Forever: A Memoir*], ed. O. Corpet & Y. M. Boutang (trans. R. Veasey). Paris: Éditions Stock/IMEC, 1994.

———— (1985b), Machiavelli. In: *L'Avenir Dure Longtemps* [*The Future Lasts Forever: A Memoir*], ed. O. Corpet & F. Matheron (trans. R. Veasey). Paris: Éditions Stock/IMEC, 1994, pp. 488–500.

———— (1998), *Lettres à Franca (1961–1973)*. Paris: Stock.

Apollon, W., Bergeron, D. & Cantin, L. (2002), *After Lacan: Clinical Practice and the Subject of the Unconscious*. Albany: State University of New York Press.

Balint, M. (1968), *The Basic Fault*. London: Tavistock.

Barzilai, S. (1999), *Lacan and the Matter of Origins*. Stanford, CA: Stanford University Press.

Bellow, S. (1953), *The Adventures of Augie March*. New York: Penguin Everyman's Library.

Borch-Jacobsen, M. (1990), *Lacan: The Absolute Master,* trans. D. Brick. Stanford, CA: Stanford University Press.

Boutang, Y. M. (1992), *Louis Althusser: Une Biographie, Tome 1*. Paris: Grasset.

———— (1997), L'interdit autobiographique et l'autorisation du livre [The biographical prohibition and authorization of the book]. In: *Lire Althusser Aujourd'hui*, ed. F. Matheron. Paris: Éditions l'Harmatton, pp. 75–113.

Bromberg, P. (1994), "Speak! That I may see you": Some reflections on dissociation, reality, and psychoanalytic listening. *Psychoanal. Dial.*, 4:517–547.

———— (1998), *Standing in the Spaces: Essays on Clinical Process, Trauma, and Dissociation*. Hillsdale, NJ: The Analytic Press.

Bucci, W. (1985), Dual coding: A cognitive model for psychoanalytic research. *J. Amer. Psychoanal. Assn.*, 33:571–607.

Camus, A. (1948), Ni victimes ni bourreaux [Neither victims nor torturers]. In: *Actuelles: Écrits Politiques*. Paris: nrf.

Clement, C. (1981), *The Lives and Legends of Jacques Lacan*, trans. A. Goldhammer. New York: Columbia University Press, 1983.

Corpet, O. & Boutang, Y. M. (1992), Présentation. In: *L'Avenir Dure Longtemps* [*The Future Lasts Forever: A Memoir*], ed. O. Corpet & Y. M. Boutang (trans. R. Veasey). Paris: Éditions Stock/IMEC, 1992, pp. 7–25.

——— & Matheron, F. (1996), Introduction. In: *Writings on Psychoanalysis*, ed. O. Corpet & F. Matheron (trans. J. Mehlman). New York: Columbia University Press, pp. 2–12.

de Marty, É. (1999), *Louis Althusser, Un Sujet Sans Procès. Anatomie d'un passé très récent* [*Louis Althusser, A subject without a trial. Anatomy of a very recent past*]. Paris: Gallimard.

de Pommier, G. (1998), *Louis du Néant. La mélancolie d'Althusser* [*Louis of Nothingness. The Melancholy of Althusser*]. Paris: Aubier.

Derrida, J. (1974), *On Grammatology*, trans. G. C. Spivak. Baltimore: Johns Hopkins University Press.

——— & Roudinesco, E. (2001), *De quoi demain* [*What about tomorrow*]. Paris: Éditions Galilée.

Diatkine, G. (1997), *Jacques Lacan*. Paris: Presses Universitaires de France.

——— (2000), Surmoi culturel [cultural super-ego]. *Bulletin de la Société Psychanalytique de Paris*, 55:79–157.

Eigen, M. (1981), The area of faith in Winnicott, Bion, and Lacan. *Internat. J. Psycho-Anal.*, 62:413–433.

Erikson, E. (1950), *Childhood and Society*. New York: Norton.

Fairbairn, W. R. D. (1943), The repression and return of bad objects. In: *Psychoanalytic Studies of the Personality*. London: Routledge & Kegan Paul, 1952, pp. 59–81.

——— (1944), Endo-psychic structure considered in terms of object relations. In: *Psychoanalytic Studies of the Personality*. London: Routledge & Kegan Paul, 1952, pp. 82–136.

Ferenczi, S. (1933), The confusion of tongues between adults and the child: The language of tenderness and passion. In: *Final Contributions to the Problems and Methods of Psychoanalysis*, ed. M. Balint. New York: Brunner/Mazel, 1980, pp. 156–167.

Fink, B. (1997), *A Clinical Introduction to Lacanian Psychoanalysis: Theory and Technique*. Cambridge: Harvard University Press.

Freud, S. (1895), Project for a scientific psychology. *Standard Edition*, 1:295-397. London: Hogarth Press, 1966.

——— (1900), An analysis of a specimen dream. *Standard Edition*, 4:106–121. London: Hogarth Press, 1953.

——— (1914), On narcissism: An introduction. *Standard Edition*, 14:67–104. London: Hogarth Press, 1957.

——— (1917), Mourning and melancholia. *Standard Edition*, 14:243–260. London: Hogarth Press, 1956.

——— (1919), "A child is being beaten": A contribution to the study of the origin of sexual perversions. *Standard Edition*, 17:175–204, London: Hogarth Press, 1955.

—— (1920), Beyond the pleasure principle. *Standard Edition*, 18:3–66. London: Hogarth Press, 1955.

—— (1921), Group psychology and the analysis of the ego. *Standard Edition*, 18:67–145. London: Hogarth Press, 1955.

—— (1933), New introductory lectures on psychoanalysis. *Standard Edition*, 22:3–184. London: Hogarth Press, 1964.

Geertz, C. (1974), On the nature of anthropological understanding. In: *Culture Theory: Essays on Mind, Self, and Emotion*, ed. R. Schweder & R. Levine. Cambridge: Cambridge University Press, pp. 123–136.

Gopnik, A. & Meltzoff, A. N. (1997), *Words, Thoughts, and Theories*. Cambridge MA: MIT Press.

Green, A. (1973), *Le Discours Vivant, la Conception Psychanalytique de l'Affect* [*Living Speech, the Psychoanalytic Conception of Affect*]. Paris: Presses Universitaires de France.

—— (1975), The analyst, symbolization, and absence, In: *On Private Madness*. London: Maresfield Library, Karnac Books, 1986, pp. 30–59.

—— (1977), Conceptions of affect. In: *On Private Madness*. London: Maresfield Library, Karnac Books, 1986, pp. 174–213.

—— (1980a), La mère morte [The dead mother]. In: *Narcissisme de Vie/Narcissisme de Mort*. Paris: Éditions de Minuit, 1983, pp. 222–253.

—— (1980b), Passions and their vicissitudes. In: *On Private Madness*. London: Maresfield Library, Karnac Books, 1986, pp. 214–253.

—— (1997), The intuition of the negative in playing and reality. *Internat. J. Psycho-Anal.*, 78:1071–1084.

—— (1999), The greening of psychoanalysis: André Green in dialogues with Gregorio Kohen. In: *The Dead Mother*, ed. G. Kohon. New York: Routledge, pp. 10–58.

Guntrip, H. (1971), *Psychoanalytic Theory, Therapy, and the Self*. New York: Basic Books.

—— (1975), My experience of analysis with Fairbairn and Winnicott. *Internat. Rev. Psycho-Anal.*, 2:145–160.

Harari, R. (2001), *Lacan's Seminar on Anxiety: An Introduction*. New York: Other Press.

Julien, P. (1985), *Pour Lire Jacques Lacan* [*To Read Jacques Lacan*]. Paris: EPEL.

Kennedy, R. (1997), On subjective organizations: Toward a theory of subject relations. *Psychoanal. Dial.*, 7:553–581.

Khan, M. (1974), *The Privacy of the Self*. New York: International Universities Press.

Kilborne, B. (2002), *Disappearing Persons, Shame and Appearance*. Albany: State University of New York Press.

Kirshner, L. (1991), The concept of the self in psychoanalytic theory and its philosophical foundations. *J. Amer. Psychoanal. Assn.*, 39:157–183.

———— (1992), The absence of the father. *J. Amer. Psychoanal. Assn.*, 40:1117–1138.

———— (1994), Trauma, the good object, and the symbolic. *Internat. J. Psycho-Anal.*, 75:235–242.

———— (1999), Toward a postmodern realism for psychoanalysis. *J. Amer. Psychoanal. Assn.*, 47:447–461.

Kohut, H. (1977), *The Restoration of the Self*. New York: International Universities Press.

———— (1987), Early stages in the formation of self-esteem. In: *The Kohut Seminars*, ed. M. Elson. New York: Norton, pp. 31–46.

Kundera, M. (1984), *The Unbearable Lightness of Being*. New York: Penguin Classics.

Kurtz, S. (1992), *All the Mothers Are One: Hindu India and the Cultural Reshaping of Psychoanalysis*. New York: Columbia University Press.

Lacan, J. (1949), The mirror stage as formative of the function of the I. In: *Écrits: A Selection*, trans. A. Sheridan. London: Tavistock, 1977, pp. 1–8.

———— (1953), The function and field of speech in psychoanalysis. In: *Écrits: A Selection*, trans. A. Sheridan. London: Tavistock, 1977, pp. 30–113.

———— (1953–1954), *The Seminar of Jacques Lacan, Book I: Freud's Papers on Technique*, ed. J-A Miller (trans. J. Forrester). Cambridge: Cambridge University Press, 1987.

———— (1954–1955), *The Seminar of Jacques Lacan, Book II: The Ego in Freud's Theory and in the Technique of Psychoanalysis*, ed. J.-A. Miller (trans. J. Forrester). Cambridge: Cambridge University Press, 1987.

———— (1955), The Freudian thing. In: *Écrits: A Selection*, trans. A. Sheridan. London: Tavistock, 1977, pp. 114–145.

———— (1955–1956), *The Seminar of Jacques Lacan Book III: The Psychoses*, ed. J.-A. Miller (trans. R. Grigg). New York: Norton.

———— (1956–1957), *Le Seminaire, Livre IV: La Relation d'Objet*. Paris: Seuil.

———— (1958), The direction of the treatment and the principles of its power. In: *Écrits: A Selection*, trans. A. Sheridan. London: Tavistock, 1977, pp. 226–280.

———— (1959–1960), *The Seminar of Jacques Lacan, Book VII: The Ethics of Psychoanalysis*, ed. J.-A. Miller (trans. D. Porter). New York: Norton, 1992.

—— (1960), The subversion of the subject and the dialetic of desire. In: *Écrits*, trans. A. Sheridan. London: Tavistock, 1977, pp. 292–325.

—— (1960–1961), *Le Seminaire, Livre VIII: Le Transfert*. Paris: Seuil.

—— (1962–1963), L'angoisse [Anxiety]. Unpublished paper.

—— (1964), *The Four Fundamental Concepts of Psychoanalysis: The Seminar of Jacques Lacan, Book XI*, trans. A. Sheridan. New York: Norton.

—— (1966), *Écrits: A Selection*, trans. A. Sheridan. London: Tavistock, 1977, pp. 30–113.

—— (1972–1973), *Encore: The Seminar of Jacques Lacan, Book XX*, ed. J.-A. Miller (trans. B. Fink). New York: Norton, 1975.

—— (1974), *Télévision*. Paris: Seuil.

Levy, R. (1973), *Tahitians: Mind and Experience in the Society Islands*. Chicago: University of Chicago Press.

Lewis, J. (1972), The Althusser case. *Marxism Today,* Jan.–Feb.:24–27, 44–49.

Little, M. (1951), Counter-transference and the patient's response to it. *Internat. J. Psycho-Anal.*, 32:32–40.

—— (1985), Winnicott working in areas where psychotic anxieties predominate: A personal record. *Free Associations*, 3:9–42.

Loewald, H. (1980), *Papers on Psychoanalysis*. New Haven: Yale University Press.

Lutz, C. (1988), *Unnatural Emotions*. Chicago: University of Chicago Press.

Matheron, F. (1995), Présentation. In: *Louis Althusser: Écrits Philosophiques et Politiques*. Paris: Stock/IMEC, pp. 5–21.

—— (1997), La récurrence du vide chez Louis Althusser [The recurrence of the void in Louis Althusser]. In: *Lire Althusser Aujourd'hui*, ed. F. Matheron. Paris: Éditions l'Harmattan, pp. 23–47.

Meyerson, P. (1981), The nature of the transactions that enhance the progressive phases of psychoanalysis. *Internat. J. Psycho-Anal.*, 62:91–103.

—— (1991), *Childhood Dialogues and the Lifting of Repression. Character Structure and Psychoanalytic Technique*. New Haven: Yale University Press.

Miller, J.-A. (1987), How psychoanalysis cures according to Lacan. *Newsletter of the Freudian Field*, 1:4–27.

Mitchell, S. (1991), Contemporary perspectives on self: Toward an integration. *Psychoanal. Dial.*, 1:121–147.

Modell, A. (1965), On having the right to a life: An aspect of the superego's development. *Internat. J. Psycho-Anal.*, 46:423–431.

—— (1968), *Object Love and Reality*. New York: International Universities Press.

—— (1980), Affects and their non-communication. *Internat. J. Psycho-Anal.*, 61:259–268.

—— (1984), *Psychoanalysis in a New Context.* New York: International Universities Press.

—— (1990), *Other Times, Other Realities: Toward a Theory of Psychoanalytic Treatment.* Cambridge, MA: Harvard University Press.

—— (1991), A confusion of tongues or whose reality is it? *Psychoanal. Quart.,* 60:227–244.

—— (1993), *The Private Self.* Cambridge, MA: Harvard University Press.

Muller, J. P. (1989), Lacan and Kohut: From imaginary to symbolic identification in the case of Mr. Z. In: *Self Psychology: Comparisons and Contrasts,* ed. W. W. Detrick & S. P. Detrick. Hillsdale, NJ: The Analytic Press, pp. 364–394.

Ogden, T. (1994), The analytic third: Working with intersubjective clinical facts. *Internat. J. Psycho-Anal.,* 75:3–19.

Ornstein, P. (1980), Self psychology and the concept of health. In: *Advances in Self Psychology,* ed. A. Goldberg. Madison CT: International Universities Press, pp. 137–160.

Phillips, A. (1988), *Winnicott.* Cambridge, MA: Harvard University Press.

Pinker, S. (2002), *The Modern Denial of Human Nature.* New York: Viking.

Putnam, H. (1981), *Reason, Truth, and History.* Cambridge: Cambridge University Press.

Rosaldo, M. (1984), Towards an anthropology of self and feeling, In: *Culture Theory: Essays on Mind, Self, and Emotion,* ed. R. Shweder & R. Levine. Cambridge: Cambridge University Press.

Roudinesco, E. (1986), *Jacques Lacan and Co.: A History of Psychoanalysis in France, 1925–1985,* trans. J. Mehlman. Chicago: University of Chicago Press, 1990.

—— (1993), *Jacques Lacan,* trans. B. Bray. New York: Columbia University Press, 1997.

Roustang, F. (1986), *Lacan: De l'équivoque à l'impasse* [*Lacan: From Equivocation to Impasse*]. Paris: Éditions de Minuit.

Rudnytsky, P. (1991), *The Psychoanalytic Vocation.* New Haven: Yale University Press.

Sartre, J.-P. (1943), *Être et le Néant* [*Being and Nothingness*]. Paris: Gallimard.

Schafer, R. (1992), *Retelling a Life: Narrative and Dialogue in Psychoanalysis.* New York: Basic Books.

Schweder, R. (1991), *Thinking Through Cultures.* Cambridge: Harvard University Press.

Sokol, A. & Bricmont, J. (1997), *Impostures Intellectuelles* [*Intellectual Deceits*]. Paris: Editions Odile Jacob.

Solomon, R. C. (1983), *In the Spirit of Hegel.* New York: Oxford University Press.

Stern, D. (1985), *The Interpersonal World of the Infant*. New York: Basic Books.

Tolpin, P. (1980), The borderline personality, its makeup and analyzability. In: *Advances in Self Psychology*, ed. A. Goldberg. New York: International Universities Press, pp. 290–299.

Vaillant, G. (1977), *Adaptation to Life*. Boston: Little, Brown.

Van Haute, P. (2002), *Against Adaptation*. New York: Other Press.

Ver Eeke, W. (1983), Hegel as Lacan's source for necessity in psychoanalytic theory. In: *Interpreting Lacan*, ed. J. Smith & W. Kerrigan. New Haven: Yale University Press, pp. 113–138.

Viderman, S. (1979), The analytic space, meaning and problems. *Psychoanal. Quart.*, 48:257–291.

Whorf, W. (1956), *Language, Thought, and Reality: Selected Writings of Benjamin Lee Whorf*. Cambridge, MA: MIT Press.

Wilden, A. (1968), *Speech and Language in Psychoanalysis*. Baltimore: Johns Hopkins University Press.

Winnicott, D. W. (1953), Transitional objects and transitional phenomena. In: *Playing and Reality*. New York: Basic Books, 1971, pp. 1–25.

—— (1954), Metapsychological and clinical aspects of regression within the psycho-analytical set-up. In: *Through Paediatrics to Psychoanalysis*. New York: Basic Books, 1975, pp. 278–294.

—— (1960), Counter-transference. In: *Essential Papers on Countertransference*, ed. B. Wolstein. New York: New York University Press, 1988, pp. 262–269.

—— (1971), *Playing and Reality*. New York: Basic Books.

—— (1973), Fear of breakdown. *Internat. Rev. Psycho-Anal.*, 1:103–107.

—— (1986), *Holding and Interpretation*. New York: Grove Press.

—— & Khan, M. M. R. (1953), Review of *Psychoanalytic Studies of the Personality*, by W. R. D. Fairbairn. *Internat. J. Psycho-Anal.*, 34:329–333.

Wolf, E. (1980), On the developmental line of selfobject relations. In: *Advances in Self Psychology*, ed. A. Goldberg. New York: International Universities Press, pp. 117–132.

Zacharias, B. L. (2002), *Strategic Marketing Initiative, American Psychoanalytic Association: Market Research Report*. The Zacharias Group.

Žižek, S. (1989), *The Sublime Object of Ideology*. London: Verso.

—— (1992), *Enjoy Your Symptom*. New York: Routledge, 2001.

—— (1994), *The Metastases of Enjoyment: Six Essays on Woman and Causality*. London: Verso.

Index

—▶ ◀—

Ricoeur, P., 140
Riviere, J., 18
Rosaldo, M., 57
   on affect, 55
Roudinesco, E., 2, 5n, 14, 16n, 17,
   17n, 23, 111
   criticism of Althusser, 137
Roustang, F., 5n, 15n
Rudnytsky, P., 9, 11, 12, 17, 24
Rytmann, Hélène, 126, 128, 131

S
Sartre, J.P., idealization of individual, 139
Saussure, F., 43
Schafer, R., 34, 59
Schweder, R., 69
   on affect, 55
   soul loss, 56–57
   vocabulary of emotion, 56
Sebag, Lucien, suicide of, 137
self, 2–3, 10–21, 33–34, 46, 66
   closeness *vs.* distance, 10
   cohesive, 32–33, 141
   conceptions of, 11–12
   differential constructions, 58–59
   discourse and, 33–34
   emptiness of, 71n
   fantasy and, 71
   narrated, 34
   negative hallucination, 10
   vs. subject, 2
self-definition, 30–31
self-restoration, 8–9
Sharpe, E.F., 9, 24
Socrates, 110
Sokol, A., 112n
Solomon, R.C., 36
Sorbonne, 125
speech
   empty and full, 35
   interpretive, 46
Spinoza, B., 140
Stern, D., 19, 30
Strachey, J., 18
subject, *vs.* self, 2
subjective existence, 6

subjectivity
   as effect of language, 29–30
   reinterpretation of, 44
symbolic dimension, 43–49
symbolic function, 47–48
symbolic identification, 120–121
symbolic order, 50–54, 67, 86–88

T
"Talk to Her" (Almodovar), 108–
   110
   object petit a, 109
tension arc
   Kohut's concept, 33–34
   pole of ideals and, 46
third, the, 44–45, 47, 53, 89–90
Tiresias, 16
Tolpin, P., 48
trauma, 100
   definition of, 76n
   repetition of unsymbolized, 87
   transmission of, 92–93
traumatic experience, symbolized,
   73
trust, 88
   basic, 89–90

U
unconscious, mobilization of, 45

V
Valery, P., on poetry, 81
Valliant, G., *Adaptation to Life*, 5
Van Haute, P., 5, 5n, 8n, 36n, 104
   point de capiton , 42n
   on treatment, 28n
Ver Ecke, W., 36n
Viderman, S.
   on analytic space, 46
   on interpretive speech, 44–45

W
Wendy (case), 114–123
   mirror transference, 123
   objet petit a, 116
   transferential relationship, 122–
   123